Zombiescapes and Phantom Zones

Zombiescapes and Phantom Zones

Ecocriticism and the Liminal from *Invisible Man* to *The Walking Dead*

LEE ROZELLE

The University of Alabama
Tuscaloosa

The University of Alabama Press
Tuscaloosa, Alabama 35487-0380
uapress.ua.edu

Hardcover edition published 2016.
Paperback edition published 2022.
eBook edition published 2016.

Typeface: Stone Serif and Stone Sans

Cover images: (top) Landfill garbage waste, © zeljkosantrac; (bottom) *Last Days*, ©wgmbh; images courtesy of iStock
Cover design: Michele Myatt Quinn

Paperback ISBN: 978-0-8173-6053-5

A previous edition of this book has been cataloged by the Library of Congress.
ISBN: 978-0-8173-1926-7 (cloth)
E-ISBN: 978-0-8173-9023-5

Contents

Illustrations

Acknowledgments

Montgomery, Alabama, might not be the very first place that comes to mind when you think *doenjang jjigae,* but luckily for my writing group "the Gump" has a respectable Korean food scene these days. Kimberly Wright, Madison Jones, and I have pored over many pages of this book while enjoying many, many plates of *bulgogi.* Without you guys this project would still be lost in limbo. As I was working on my book prospectus for the University of Alabama Press, I reached out to SueEllen Campbell, Nicholas Lawrence, and Lance Newman for advice, and I sincerely appreciate them for taking the time to offer their wisdom and guidance. I would also like to thank Jamie King and Alesha Dawson for help with research and photocopying, as well as Montevallo undergraduate Sylvan Baker for indexing. Special appreciation goes out to Brian Becker and David Good for, hopefully, still being my pals after I neglected them for years to write this book.

At SAMLA 2014 I hosted a panel titled "Reanimate Earth: Liminality and *Communitas* in Literature of the Americas," and the vigorous discussion that ensued convinced me that environmental liminality was a notion worth exploring further. I appreciate everyone who took part in that marvelous session. Parts of chapter 2 were published in *South Central Review* and *Studies in the Novel,* and an early version of the Margaret Atwood section of chapter 4 was published in *Canadian Literature.* My gratitude goes out to the editors and reviewers of these journals. Thanks also to the organizers, chairs, panelists, and audience members of the following conferences for their support and feedback during presentations and plenaries that contributed to this book: the 10th Annual New Voices Conference at Georgia State University; the ASLE-UK First Biennial Graduate Conference at the University of Glasgow; the Human-Animal Boundary Symposium in Mayagüez, Puerto Rico; the NEXUS Greenways Conference in Knoxville; the Colorado Mesa University Conference on Globalization and the Environment in Grand Junction; the Southern Humanities Council Conference in Savannah; Environmental Utterance at University College Falmouth, UK; the College English Association Conference in St. Petersburg, Florida; the American Comparative Literature Association Conference 2010 in New Orleans; and ASLE 2009 at the University of Victoria, British Columbia.

Dan Waterman is a nimble, gracious editor, and I am delighted to have another opportunity to work with Dan and everyone at the University of Alabama Press. I owe a great debt to Kathleen Morgan as well for getting my first book, *Ecosublime*, into the right hands back when I was a tremulous assistant professor. Many thanks to the faculty, staff, and students at the University of Montevallo for their continued support, friendship, and travel funding. Ken Watson, my mentor at the University of Southern Mississippi, has died, so I hope for his sake he was wrong about the whole existential-meaninglessness-of-the-universe thing. Adored by an entourage of English majors and always so full of wit and literary brilliance, he had little idea what a great impact his classes had on us. Existential void or no, Ken, we miss you. Finally, let's have a rousing round of applause for my wife Kelly and our little monster, Lily. You two keep me optimistic about the future.

Abbreviations

IM	Ellison, Ralph. *Invisible Man.*
M	Atwood, Margaret. *MaddAddam.*
MD	Pynchon, Thomas. *Mason & Dixon.*
O	Walcott, Derek. *Omeros.*
OC	Atwood, Margaret. *Oryx and Crake.*
OHYS	García Márquez, Gabriel. *One Hundred Years of Solitude.*
WD	Kirkman, Robert. *The Walking Dead Compendium One.*
YF	Atwood, Margaret. *The Year of the Flood.*

Introduction

This book chronicles the weirdest, ugliest, and most mixed-up characters to appear on the literary scene since World War II, creatures intimately linked to damaged habitats that rise from the muck not to destroy or rule the world, but to save it. Golems, serpent women, zombies, and dragons emerge in these chapters alongside a horde of hybridized beings, to include humanoid animals, posthuman grotesques, and sentient landscapes. In the imaginary worlds where these curiosities roam, people and other life-forms become monsters, while aberrant, out-of-place, and unclassified bodies fashion new habitats in the face of apocalyptic dread. This book asks, "What happens to a habitat *after* its destruction? What monsters and magic rise in the gap between nostalgia and apocalyptic dreams?" Since the Trinity test of the atomic bomb in 1945,[1] these questions have inspired the greatest literary minds of the Western Hemisphere, compelling renowned writers from Canada, the United States, the Caribbean, and Latin America to write sprawling, panoramic works that not only reproach western culture for its environmental missteps but also find optimism in the face of despair. Exploring "modes of writing in which possibilities for the new are blasted from the decaying ruins of the present" (Sandilands 40), this book challenges readers to reexamine our literary wastelands to reclaim places left devastated in the past and to preserve the planet's treasured sites of biodiversity.

To imaginatively reassemble gravely damaged spaces throughout the New World, the ambitious and celebrated works of literature explored in this book invite readers to experience the contemporary landscape as if we had never seen it before. We are challenged by these authors to look at dead and forgotten places as if we were unburdened by nostalgia or dread, untouched by denial or delusion, untainted by futility or expectation. This is hard, because the disposed and discarded world can be so ugly. Think miles of dated strip mall, a hardwood forest clear-cut, or abandoned factory buildings at the edge of a dying town. Think entire neighborhoods left rotting due to flood. The authors studied here dare us to not run from the monster but to embrace, love, and even celebrate the monster. This notion will strike some ecocritics as a sellout, because to go so far as to "celebrate" lands destroyed by centuries of human misuse might be seen as a justification for further environmental destruction, a capitulation to the status quo. I believe that instead of rationalizing or fighting what's already happened, we must attain a level of acceptance that will allow the contemporary West to see our "blasted" landscapes as home, places that are even now shifting, evolving, and ever returning to the whole. "Blasted landscapes are what we have," Anna Lowenhaupt Tsing observes in *The Multispecies Salon* (2014), "and we need to explore their life-promoting patches" (108). Embracing the monster and exploring its features, this book contends, will give environmental communities new chances to flourish. Monsters reject the norms and classifications of the world that made them, and they are disturbing reminders of what we've done. The language of monstrosity and the grotesque already pervades the global discussion over the natural environment, so it's time to look closer at our dark places for what they bring.

Despite variations in geography, nationality, and culture, one finds remarkable similarities in how the authors studied in this book reimagine marred and forgotten regions in the Western Hemisphere. Gabriel García Márquez's *One Hundred Years of Solitude* (1967) and Karen Tei Yamashita's *Tropic of Orange* (1997) use magical realism, the carnivalesque, and fruit production to get beyond globalism in Latin America, while Thomas Pynchon's *Mason & Dixon* (1997) and Don DeLillo's *Underworld* (1997) sketch monstrosities and maps to reclaim US border regions. Ralph Ellison's *Invisible Man* (1952) and Derek Walcott's *Omeros* (1990) depict literary figures "going under" to find home in hegemonic spaces, and Margaret Atwood's MaddAddam trilogy (2003-2013) and the graphic series *The Walking Dead* (2004-) reassemble posthuman bodies and landscapes in journeys beyond The End. These works exemplify a larger shift in the wake of World War II and the age of global environmental disaster, one that uses narrative to reverse the flood of energies leading to environmental injustice, a widening wealth gap, mass toxification, and the breakdown of material infrastructures.

Writing from a variety of national and ethnic traditions, these authors remind us that landscape is ideology in transit, which means that our broken lands are both the by-products and architects of psychospatial transformation. Community projects such as the bicycle transit system in Chattanooga, Tennessee, respond to resource depletion and congestion as they remap ideology onto outmoded urban structures to conjure up an improbable boundary region and place of magic. The daring bikers who don plastic helmets and pedal between the curb and lines of clattering pickup trucks, freewheeling retirees, and zigzagging SUVs in downtown Chattanooga find themselves at a special crossroads, because being at such eco-political boundaries "affords human beings moments of reflection about possibilities, that is, the opportunity for ecotopian dreaming about alternative arrangements of the environment" (Nattermann 114). Similarly, the literary and cultural artifacts highlighted in this book dwell within a terra incognita that is dangerous, multiple, and teeming with possibility. These zones and their inhabitants are associated with the reversibility and blurring of geographical edges; figures in these books often find themselves immersed in difficult journeys, feeling homesick, reconsidering place identity, negotiating vexed topographies, and undergoing all sorts of reanimation. All dwell in what anthropologist Victor Turner calls a "fruitful darkness" (*Forest* 110), in places like landfills, islands (concrete and otherwise), toxic waste dumps, deserted urban boroughs, tourist traps, and test sites. I believe that thinking seriously about America's badlands will help us recognize that even our most abject spaces have the capacity to reach Tom Moylan's "critical utopia" (11), places "imperfect and in process" that don't give a "blueprint for the ideal society" but offer instead a "rich blending of creative fantasy, critical thinking, and oppositional activism" (Barnhill 214). There's new growth in the twentieth-century cracks, and reasons surely abound for the environmental movement to be optimistic about the future of life. Even in the aftermath of the Deepwater Horizon, Hurricane Katrina, and Superstorm Sandy. After droughts in Argentina, wildfires in California, and floods in Alberta. After the publication of "Global Warming Preceded by Increasing Carbon Dioxide Concentrations during the Last Deglaciation." Even now, as the new climate accord is unveiled in Paris, there are reasons to be optimistic. Though Greg Garrard admits that the "despair engendered by modernity seems to demand an apocalyptic resolution" (91), he reasons that the "real moral and political challenge of ecology may lie in accepting that the world is not about to end, that human beings are likely to survive even if Western-style civilization does not. Only if we imagine that the planet has a future, after all, are we likely to take responsibility for it" (107). The world isn't coming to an end, Garrard suggests, but future generations in the West perhaps shouldn't bank on all the creature comforts of middle-class life. Garrard also implies that American literary history reveals far more than a one-way street to ecocide, that the narrative describing linear movement from purity to corruption—particularly under the auspices of crisis—fails to sufficiently consider damaged and abandoned sites that still hold ecological promise. This book is therefore not about a return to the past; Timothy Morton is right that we "simply can't unthink modernity" and that if "there is any enchantment, it lies in the future" (*Ecological* 104). Rather than simply bemoaning losses, the authors studied in this book seek to re-enchant readers with places already polluted, forgotten, or left for dead. Of course, this re-enchantment can be successful only if we move beyond lingering Euro-American attitudes that fail to incorporate black, brown, and indigenous understandings of spatial bodies in the Western Hemisphere.[2] To better characterize the social and biological communities that emerge in these works, this book adopts an indigenous "vision of progress that does not depend on the concepts of linear time and taxonomized individuals" (Sharp, "Questing" 21) as it subverts colonialist horror stories that depict racialized, species-oriented, and sexual contraventions as markers of "the end of the world." Rather, this book seeks not modern apocalypse or wasteland but a condition akin to the Ojibwe state of *bimaadiziwin*, which is the "state of balance, one of difference of provisionality, a condition of resistance and survival" (Dillon 9). Drawing from more hopeful Native American apocalyptic visions, this book "shows the ruptures, the scars and the trauma [of ecological destruction] in its effort ultimately to provide healing and a return to *bimaadiziwin*" (9) or *communitas*.

Another important step to giving disturbed places reconsideration is to complicate the socially engendered "margin," "border," and much-theorized "boundary."[3] While having proven important to studies of gender and race, these terms do not sufficiently encompass physical terrain in millennial, transnational contexts. Ursula K. Heise recognizes that the "ecocritical lack of engagement with theories of globalization and transnationalism has begun to be recognized as a challenge for the field" ("Ecocriticism" 387), and Morton agrees that "ecological thought cannot abide national boundaries" (*Ecological* 51). Lawrence Buell suggests that one way "environmental writing . . . intervenes most powerfully within and against standard conceptions of spatial apportionment is by challenging assumptions about border and scale" (*Future* 76-77), and Patrick D. Murphy fittingly states that the "envisioning of allonational formations—alternatives to the nation-state—in imaginative literature provides an important arena for debating and conceptualizing green alternatives to the modern corporate state" (*Ecocritical* 76). Rethinking literary environments with this expanded vision, this book foregrounds spatial reapportionment by shedding conceptions of national boundary and approaching landscapes throughout the Americas, particularly those abject or forgotten, as *limen*. The liminal—a concept typically associated with anthropology or psychoanalysis—can spark new connections between human culture and its more anomalous literary environments. Undoubtedly, western literature in the second half of the twentieth century has depicted its more monstrous territories' capacities for reanimation with growing urgency and imagination.

Such meditations in Latin American literature can be found in works ranging from Mexican author Juan Rulfo's *Pedro Páramo* (1955) to *The Arrivants* by Caribbean poet Kamau Brathwaite (1973) and Chilean novelist Isabel Allende's *Island Beneath the Sea* (2011). Canadian author Michael Ondaatje's *The Collected Works of Billy the Kid* (1996) returns to the liminal edge, as do Thomas King's *Green Grass, Running Water* (1993) and films such as *The Brood* (1979) and *Naked Lunch* (1991) by Canadian filmmaker David Cronenberg. William T. Vollmann's *Seven Dreams* series (1990-) should be included in this inventory alongside modern classic *The Road* (2007) by Cormack McCarthy and popular fantasy "The Dark Tower" series by Stephen King, as might movies ranging from pod-heavy science-fiction feature *Silent Running* (1972) to documentary *An Inconvenient Truth* (2006) and zombie blockbuster *World War Z* (2013). These works and countless others throughout the Western Hemisphere speak to border regions in the liminal stage to foster new intellectual approaches to rapidly changing landscapes in a climate of increasing uncertainty.

But what might a "limen" look like? As genera "betwixt and between," liminal bodies are "frequently likened to death, to being in the womb, to invisibility, to darkness, to bisexuality, to the wilderness, and to an eclipse of the sun or moon" (Turner, *Ritual* 95). As creatures in environmental limbo, the gigantic golems and dragons in *Mason & Dixon* live in a literary biosphere with the Crakers and genetically engineered pigoons of *Oryx and Crake*, zombies in *The Walking Dead*, the pigtailed babies of *One Hundred Years of Solitude*, Arcangel and Rafaela the snake woman in *Tropic of Orange*, Jack-the-Bear in *Invisible Man*, Achille the fish-man in *Omeros*, and the misshapen fetuses of *Underworld*. These "chimerical figurations" are not-so-distant cousins to Jill H. Casid's centaur, which is described in *Environmental Criticism for the Twenty-First Century* (2011) as "not a figure of stable hybridity but a roving, even rogue body that moves out of protective or controlling enclosure, traversing, overturning, and even destroying boundaries such as the fence between human and animal to an as yet unimagined and undefined space of future conceptions and consequence" (62). It is my hope that this book will help to define our spatial centaurs not as static hybrids or corroded old cyborgs but as liminal bodies that participate in elaborate ecosocial rituals of death and rebirth.

Subsequently, monster bodies in all of these works become nodes of contention in the struggle over natural environments throughout the Americas. Humanoid morphology is therefore an entry point for a larger meditation on the interplay between self and ecosystem to remind us that when life-forms morph to embody other forms, they can't stay separate from the outside. When human identities in limbo can no longer remain limited to the thinking me, the mutual or symbiotic self appears.[4] Key for the literary works studied in this book is the recognition that this mutualism is not restricted to the living; the self transmogrifies to become not only nonhuman life but also terrain. Thus, in the following chapters one finds a direct correlation between the grotesque body and the damaged earth, which makes liminal entities—humans, objects, and places—effectively one. As damaged parts of a symbiotic whole, all must go through difficult rites of passage together to find home. Both Buendía family and Macondo must experience a century of solitude before the novel's portentous storm, just as Rafaela and Los Angeles must converge with the Tropic of Cancer. Pynchon's Mason and Dixon must walk the line as the waste managers in DeLillo's novel delve deep into the underworld. The Invisible Man migrates from Deep South to Harlem to find his urban place of hibernation, while "Walcott" must travel the world to finally go native in St. Lucia. Survivors in *The Walking Dead* and the MaddAddam trilogy alike must go on epic journeys to seek novel habitats in the wake of apocalypse. In each instance traveler and environment together experience the liminal in allegorical rites.

Arnold van Gennep's seminal work *The Rites of Passage* explains that transitional or liminal entities are "outside society, and society has no power over them . . . and [are] therefore untouchable and dangerous" (114). For both Gennep and Turner, initiates in rites of passage must go through three basic stages: separation, limen, and reincorporation.[5] Turner characterizes the liminal stage as an "interval, however brief, of margin or limen, when the past is momentarily negated, suspended or abrogated, and the future has not yet begun, an instant of pure potentiality" (*Ritual* 44). After detachment the liminar defies both normalization and aesthetic appropriation to enter a temporal threshold in flux. For the larger structural body, the liminar often becomes unsightly, as the rejection of designation makes him/her/it/them an inadvertent threat or nuisance. Turner adds that as well as the "betwixt-and-between state of liminality there is the state of outsiderhood," which sets the unsightly one "outside the structural arrangements of a given social system" (*Dramas* 232–33). The liminal being enters a state of uncertainty that is "not only a form of transition but also a potentiality" (Spariosu 33); this is the "indescribable time when the individual has left the past but has not yet arrived at his/her destination" (qtd. in Brooker 13). The third stage, reincorporation, involves what Turner deems *communitas*. At this place and time, the transmuted limen and the shaken culture have a window of opportunity to rejoin and form a more stable, complex state.

The possibilities for this concept are tremendous for ecocriticism when we perceive the liminal self as *place*. As limen the zombiescapes and phantom zones depicted in post–World War II literature become catalysts for environmental reanimation and sources of hope.

This book therefore focuses on literary works from 1950 to 2015 that breathe new life into dead zones and brownfields[6] that have been divested of much of their biodiversity and ecological viability. What I am proposing is the observance, sorting, and wise use of declassified lands where it will take more than reforestation and revegetation to make things right again. Sites of interest might include interstate medians, abandoned military posts, places either flooded or desertified by climate change, tornado-ravaged towns, strip mines, strip malls, college campuses, and even graveyards where orchards might grow. With this goal in mind, the conservation ethic of first-wave ecocriticism can be bolstered to make the Western Hemisphere more biophilic and sustainable. By making post-ecological spaces like abandoned superstore backlots and missile test sites more biologically complex, paradise lost can support the health and well-being of extant biota that remains. Key to this book is the understanding that liminality is not a condition but a phase, which means that though a gravely damaged area can "never be reconstituted in its original diversity" (Wilson, *Biophilia* 121), as E. O. Wilson acknowledges, it can still serve to offset damage already done. It can reach *communitas.* As the following chapters show, liminal spaces can reduce the effects of pollution, promote environmental justice, lessen economic disparities, and localize food production. These zones and bodies also promote nonhuman rights and unsettle neocolonialist or depletionist mind-sets.[7] In limbo easy political positions fall away, along with the unquestioned eminence of the global Googlopolis, with its constant stream of marketable techneologisms. As ecocritics and stewards of the earth, we must look outside again, and again, rename what we witness, see it as another thing, and lovingly recover even the ugliest remnants of our heedless past.

With these values in mind, this project aims to advance the ecocritical conversation in a number of anticipated ways. If "ecocriticism is to have any real force as a theoretical and pedagogical approach," suggest the editors of *Beyond Nature Writing: Expanding the Boundaries of Ecocriticism* (2001), "ecocritics need to attend to [altered] landscapes" by "reading texts set in environments profoundly and clearly altered by humans" (Armbruster and Wallace 6). In *The Future of Environmental Criticism* (2005), Buell identifies the need for more study of post-ecological spaces but recognizes that "at least we are starting to see the beginning of incorporation of urban and other severely altered, damaged landscapes—'brownfields' as well as greenfields—into ecocriticism's accounts of placeness and place-attachment. For ecocriticism to recognize" the brownfield as "something other than non-place is itself a great and necessary advance" (88).[8] In literary theory, Timothy Morton's *Ecology Without Nature* (2007) and *The Ecological Thought* (2010) interrogate stultifying and outmoded conceptions of place for the sake of renewal. Attractive for my argument is Morton's desire to go dark, so that we might rethink our "naïve concept of interconnectedness" (*Ecology* 200) and better prepare for the crisis-ridden and depleted landscapes that seethe behind aesthetic beauty and corporatist symmetry. Importantly, Morton stresses that we should be "nostalgic for the future, helping people figure out that the ecological 'paradise' *has not occurred yet*" (162). And though Morton's books give only a glimmer of what this paradise might look like in practice, he reframes the conversation significantly by explaining that literature provides a "potential space, a limbo waiting to generate value" (86) and maintains that "we *cannot* go on thinking of [liminal beings] as 'in between'" (51). My work explores this "potential space," this "limbo," to offer ecocriticism ways to find value and meaning within and beyond our interstitial regions.

As environmental literary criticism continues to evolve as a discipline, I can't quite embrace the impulse to let go of first-wave methodologies and practices that draw inspiration from the natural sciences. If ecocriticism is to remain relevant outside the arts and humanities, science must continue to provide the principal source of inspiration and knowledge for the humanities in its desire to go green. Ecology without nature is dandy, but ecocriticism without science is dangerous.[9] And while it's true that most ecocritics like myself have primary expertise in the arts and humanities, we have an obligation to get as close as we can to understanding the biology, chemistry, geology, and other disciplines that found our readings, theories, and speculations. If asked to describe global warming or estuarine ecosystems, I have to admit, I could come up with only rudimentary explanations based more on websites and soundbites than peer-reviewed scientific journals and comprehensive studies. Within the burgeoning ecocritical community I am not alone in this. But acknowledging my status as layperson in the sciences gives me, an emissary from the humanities, the obligation to stay as current as possible in my understanding of ecology so that my own area of expertise might offer something of value.

To return to Turner's thesis and the question left for contemporary ecocriticism: what might *communitas* in the Western Hemisphere look like? The literary and cultural artifacts studied in this book provide an array of suggestions for bringing our liminal monsters and disfigured lands back from the grave. The editors of *Environmental Criticism for the Twenty-First Century* write that contemporary environmental literary critics are actively "in search of adequate spatial frameworks to understand how literature and the arts engage processes such as the loss of ice from polar ice sheets; the stagnations and movements of entities like oil around the planet; or the unevenly related genealogies of thought that authors often gather together to frame the environment" (LeMenager, Shewry, and Hiltner 12). This book offers liminality as one such spatial framework so that the space of distortion might become a place where revelation and advocacy are possible again; the grotesques that ooze and crawl from these chapters challenge readers to consider new ways to reinhabit our zombiescapes and phantom zones at a time when energy efficiency, fracking, climate, Pacific trade, local food, and sustainability shape the intellectual landscape. The editors of *The Bioregional Imagination* offer "[r]einhabitory practices" not simply "to be able to sustain the current circumstances, but to find ways of living that repair the environmental harm caused by previous behavior," practices such as "founding remanufacturing businesses to make new products from byproducts and discarded materials, retrofitting homes to conserve energy, or, better yet, to produce energy, converting brownfields to gardens . . . and even reimagining what a bioregionally inspired local literary tradition might consist of" (Lynch, Glotfelty, and Armbruster 6). I wholeheartedly agree. But to get to the place where American culture can adopt stewardship as life practice, the core of any bioregionally inspired retrofit must be prepared to embrace the paradox of hope in ruins.

Liminality gives ecocriticism exciting and useful new ways to conceptualize landscapes that have historically proven troublesome, unwieldy, and hard to define. But ecocritics will find much more within these chapters. In chapter 1 García Márquez offers environmental literary criticism a "bioregionalist manifesto" in his cautionary tale of incest and international trade; Yamashita advances these motifs and concepts to spurn NAFTA and promote sustainable urbanities as part of a larger transnational *Weltanschauung*. Chapter 2 examines Pynchon's Mason-Dixon Line as well as DeLillo's waste and warheads to interrogate the ontology of colonized space and unsettle the boundaries of military superpower. Ellison in chapter 3 demands environmental justice for dispossessed African Americans, while Walcott promotes an ecological awakening in the Caribbean that rejects the economic foundations of ecosocial hegemony. In chapter 4 Kirkman's apocalyptic narrative advances animal rights, local food production, and nonhierarchical thinking; Atwood's apocalypse similarly offers a survivor's ethos that compels readers to think beyond global warming, human overpopulation, and the mutability of humankind. These works provide an ecocritical platform that is at once intellectually transnational, economically bioregional, and environmentally sustainable. Perhaps most important for environmental literary criticism, the authors studied here inaugurate liminality as a continual process. They remind us that bodies and communities in this dark carnival interminably experience the agonies and joys of rebirth. Place, we find, is always being born.

1
A Fruitful Darkness

Bioregional Grotesques in Gabriel García Márquez's *One Hundred Years of Solitude* and Karen Tei Yamashita's *Tropic of Orange*

After disasters like the historic tornado outbreak of April 2011, there's this strange feeling of frenzied desolation, a dissonance created by battered towns and woodlands that scarcely resemble the places they were. For a time helicopters hover overhead, chainsaws cut along roadways, and power lines hang in tree limbs. People and vehicles move in and out of the ruin. All around one experiences suffering, emotional overload, and exhaustion. Lines of worn-out people wait for electricity and news as the civil infrastructure sputters. And the land during this period becomes three places at once: the home we remember, the wrecked thing it is, and the new place. This strange and shifting terrain can be found wherever a tropical storm hits a town, a wildfire destroys a neighborhood, an unseasonable flood rises above the sandbags, or a drought kills off a farmer's crops. Wherever the drastic effects of human-induced climate change can be felt, liminality blooms in its wake to offer humanity both tragedy and another chance to reflect. It is difficult for the writer of fiction to do these places justice, because the tension and drama too often get choked with stale action, syrupy pathos, or apocalyptic fantasy. But in the winged hands of Gabriel García Márquez, even catastrophe thrives with wonders. In *One Hundred Years of Solitude* and a handful of works by talented literary successors such as Karen Tei Yamashita, magical realism and the carnivalesque are used in Latin American settings to characterize the simultaneous push and pull of catastrophe and redemption, isolation and international trade, economic coercion and social upheaval, tradition and modern advance. Both *One Hundred Years of Solitude* and *Tropic of Orange* focus on Latin American homes and gardens to examine the impact of bioregional damage on families, and both meditate on fruit production to show the effects of international trade on native communities. Shapeshifters in both books conflate human bodies and other forms to create a veritable circus of geographical oddities where places transition magically into new states of being.

Nuevo Mundo

Among its many other literary feats, *One Hundred Years of Solitude* manages to be nothing short of a bioregionalist manifesto, a "work of ecological wisdom" (R. Williams 75) that compels readers to both accept parameters set by biological networks and prize regional identity. Feelings of isolation and solitude in García Márquez's masterpiece come from a loss of local vision and the kaleidoscopic effects of rapid economic and political change in Latin America throughout the twentieth century. In 1927, when García Márquez was born in the Caribbean department of Magdalena, the coastal economy already "consisted of much more than old-style cattle ranches. Commercial production of tobacco and sugar, small-scale productions of foodstuffs for urban centers, and the multiplier effects of the banana enclave, all generated new regional dynamics" (Palacios 53). Little Gabito grew up at a time when Colombia and other Latin American nations were becoming modern states, developing rail and highway systems, and edging into the international marketplace. Solitude in this context becomes much more than a "psychological, social, and cultural condition"; it is, to quote Ursula K. Heise, also "an ecological condition, an index of the deterritorialization individuals and communities experience even in relation to their most immediate natural surroundings" ("Local" 142). Carnival, a phantasmagoric recurring cycle of spectacle and exchange, introduces intercontinental trade to Magdalena, and thus to literary Macondo. With carny spectacle come pseudoscience, magic, erotic taboo, and a funhouse of mechanical diversions. After the novel's Melquíades brings the magnet and other marvels to a world "so recent that many things lacked names" (*OHYS* 1), Macondo becomes a *costeño* portal where bodies and landscapes experience transformation as liminal beings, which causes the region and its inhabitants to find themselves for a time "physically and magico-religiously in a special situation" (Gennep 18). García Márquez's phantasmic *nuevo mundo* functions only intermittently within the laws of physics and becomes a freewheeling arena where plants, animals, vegetation, and climate get mixed up in the lives of human inhabitants. The citizens of Macondo who successfully negotiate this American terrain, the novel suggests, are those who keep their bearings and maintain independence from encroaching global commerce in its various guises.

If the Buendías Had Listened

Melquíades and the Romany gypsies are the first in a long line of allegorical figures that introduce international trade to Macondo. Inhabitants of the isolated town, people with little experience with scientific gadgets, imaginatively transform the magnet and the telescope into instruments of magic. The introduction of science as spectacle clouds Macondo's vision of the physical world and allows for various missteps that seal the Buendía family's fate. Though the opening pages of *One Hundred Years of Solitude* seem to waver between nostalgia and the limits of isolation, it doesn't take the reader long to realize that the novel champions matriarch Úrsula's practice of maintaining connections to the province and resisting the hype surrounding hegemonic European and US enterprises. Mesmerized by the lure of (pseudo)science, on the other hand, José Arcadio Buendía loses touch with his bioregional imagination. Before he loses it, José Arcadio Buendía founds a Macondo that for a while is "orderly and hardworking" and "a truly happy village" (*OHYS* 9). He arranges the "houses in such a way that from all of them one could reach the river and draw water with the same effort" and lines up "the streets with such good sense that no house got more sun than another during the hot time of the day" (9). Unfortunately, his "spirit of social initiative" disappears when he is "pulled away by the fever of the magnets, the astronomical calculations, the dreams of transmutation, and the urge to discover the wonders of the world" (9). Gustavo Llarull agrees that the founder's tragic blunder is that he becomes isolated from "social interaction and ethical guidance" (97), and Brian Conniff adds that his "view of the world shares too much with the oppressors who will take over his village in the delirium of banana fever" (145). Iris M. Zavala goes further to show that José Arcadio Buendía and Colombians like him who "seek the route of the Anglo-Saxon North for the sake of utility and progress will only lead us to the oppression of speculators and capitalists who . . . proceed to wring us dry" (122). As José Arcadio Buendía spends money on contraptions and tests various outlandish theories in seclusion, "Úrsula and the children [break] their backs in the garden, growing banana and caladium, cassava and yams, ahuyama roots and eggplants" (*OHYS* 4). García Márquez contrasts the indulgences of José Arcadio Buendía—practices that will curse his offspring to a century of trauma and despair—with Úrsula's common sense, sustainable ethos, and social awareness.

Eminent García Márquez scholar Gene H. Bell-Villada writes that the "rain of yellow flowers at the founder's death represents all Nature mourning for a great man . . . a theme common enough in world myths" (*García* 112). But a biocentric reading with Conniff's and Zavala's arguments in mind would suggest that nature here does not mourn for José Arcadio Buendía; rather, the natural ecosystem weeps flowers for Macondo as it foretells a century of destruction brought about in a protracted boom-bust cycle. I liken the yellow rain to confetti, which means that the natural world surrounding Macondo is actually celebrating. The "silent storm" that accompanies the death of José Arcadio Buendía is described as having "covered the roofs and blocked the doors and smothered the animals who slept outdoors" (*OHYS* 140). Yellow in this passage represents mourning, but it also means gold, the family wealth that will over time both shower and smother the Buendías as well. Bell-Villada explains that García Márquez "skillfully reimagines his New World history, casting the descendants of Spanish settlers in the role of indigenes being encroached upon by royal bureaucrats, proselytizing priests, and Yankee capitalists, all of whom wish to absorb a peaceable Macondo into their vast global schemes" (*García* 116). From this standpoint, *One Hundred Years of Solitude* does not simply advocate isolationist policies for Colombia, Cuba, and other Latin American nations. What it calls for instead is bioregional inspiration to negotiate the country's dizzying cultural, religious, and economic shifts. It is this inspiration that Yamashita will champion in *Tropic of Orange* to foster indigenous and sustainable practices in the wake of NAFTA.

The area surrounding Macondo is described as a distinct bioregion because it shares commonalities of nonhuman life and topography where borders are determined by geographical features. Though the town itself is modeled after Aracataca, its borders are more suggestive of the nearby town of Sucre, where García Márquez spent time as a youth. Sucre is described in Gerald Martin's *Gabriel García Márquez: A Life* (2009) as a "floating island lost in a lattice-work of rivers and streams amidst what had once been dense tropical jungle" in a landscape "constantly changing and shifting between scrub forest and savannah, depending on the season and the height of the rivers" (67). José Arcadio Buendía, who is described as "completely ignorant of the geography of the region" (*OHYS* 10), characterizes the area surrounding Macondo by its very inaccessibility, with the Caribbean to the north and west and "an impenetrable [Sierra Nevada] mountain chain" to the east. To the south, it is believed, "lay the swamps, covered with an eternal vegetable scum, and the whole vast universe of the great swamp, which, according to the gypsies, had no limits. The great swamp in the west mingled with the boundless extension of water" (10). Like Sucre, Macondo is framed on all sides by well-defined parameters, but with seemingly endless boundaries. Its edges are imbued with preternatural fecundity and life-forms both sentient and divine that transport the townspeople to states of spectral bewilderment.

When José Arcadio Buendía and his party first explore the area, they find themselves unable to "return because the strip that they were opening as they went along would soon close up with a new vegetation that almost seemed to grow before their eyes" (11). From the beginning, natural environment is a motivating force that directs the action in *One Hundred Years of Solitude*, a dynamism that guides, rewards, and punishes the Buendías to the end of the line. When founded, Macondo is a fertile region blessed with a clean water source, good soil, edible vegetation, and diverse wildlife, such as numerous bird species. But as the profligate Buendías abuse their power and resources, Macondo becomes less and less familiar to them. In this way Macondo truly becomes a city with "mirror walls" (24), a symbolic region that reflects choices and policies made on behalf of misguided municipalities throughout the Americas, then and now. But this parable of place leaves many questions as yet unanswered by the scholarship: What is the natural world trying to teach the Buendías and readers across the Western Hemisphere in regard to our own liminal landscapes? What would Macondo have looked like if the Buendías had listened? How should we throughout the Americas apply Macondo's lessons in the twenty-first century?

Beastly Beasts

Human-animal relations offer clues as to how the questions above might be answered, as this novel keeps returning to the murky, shifting line between *Homo sapiens* and other species. Importantly, the liminal stage in Macondo's rite of passage is wrought with "profuse symbolic reference to beasts, birds, and vegetation" (Turner, *Dramas* 252), because in *One Hundred Years of Solitude* "life is snuffed out by animality and nature, even as it is being regenerated by these very same forces" (253). Macondo is not unlike García Márquez's own characterization of New York as zombiescape: a place "putrefying" but "also in the process of rebirth" (Kennedy 258). The novel illustrates this paradox by depicting human creatures that become entangled with spiders, insects, weeds, mythical chimeras, suggestive flowers, and erratic climes as well as incestuous kin. Early in the book we see one such limen at the edge of the "great swamp" that "mingles" with the Caribbean Sea, creatures described as "soft-skinned cetaceans that had the head and torso of a woman, causing the ruination of sailors with the charm of their extraordinary breasts" (*OHYS* 10). García Márquez brilliantly makes the connection between estuarine ecosystems—fertile transitional zones where freshwater and seawater mingle—and the crossbred offspring of human and dolphin. The lure of intercourse between and among ecological participants in a veritable orgy of species stimulates feelings of magnetism and threat. By giving evolutionary biology a human face, García Márquez explores the sex act as threshold experience that intermingles body parts, genetic materials, and biomes in liminal unrest. Such bodies in Macondo require readers to "acknowledge the monstrosity at the heart of the idea of nature" (Morton, *Ecology* 195) and to also demand as a matter of survival the imaginative construction of its sustainable mirror image. Úrsula is convinced that a child born of incest will have a pig's tail, José Arcadio Buendía responds that if "you bear iguanas, we'll raise iguanas" (*OHYS* 22), and enraged Prudencio Aguilar taunts José Arcadio Buendía by suggesting, "Maybe that rooster of yours can do your wife a favor" (21). Animals become fetishistic totems that embody dark desires and the conception of ecological grotesques.[1]

The compulsion to commit incest in *One Hundred Years of Solitude* is part of a larger taboo that arises in Macondo's liminal phase. For García Márquez, ecological destruction and cultural taboo become the same act when they cannibalize Macondo for decadent pleasures and personal affluence. Aureliano Segundo, for example, becomes extravagantly wealthy because of the "supernatural proliferation of his animals. His mares would bear triplets, his hens laid twice a day, and his hogs fattened with such speed that no one could explain such disorderly fecundity" (189). He believes that intercourse with his concubine Petra Cotes has spawned the "irremediable plague of proliferation" (190) that infects his breeding grounds. But rather than conserve part of his wealth as Úrsula instructs, he, during wild debauches, uncorks "champagne just for the pleasure of pouring the foam over his head" (191); it is told that there "was a slaughtering of so many cows, pigs, and chickens for the endless parties that the ground of the courtyard turned black and muddy with so much blood" (255). The courtyard becomes an "eternal execution ground of bones and innards, a mud pit of leftovers, and they had to keep exploding dynamite bombs all the time so that buzzards would not pluck out the guests' eyes" (255). The hellish imagery in these passages transforms Macondo into "execution ground" and site of sexual exploitation, while the unscrupulous butchery of animals likens family courtyard to *desolladero.* Correspondingly, Aureliano Segundo's own body becomes "fat, purple-colored [and] turtle shaped" (255), his morphology reptilian and bloated, an abject mirror image of the "totemic female" deemed "The Elephant" with whom he has an eating contest during the festivities. After eating thirty raw eggs, two pigs, a bunch of bananas, and way-too-much turkey, he falls "facedown into the plate filled with bones, frothing at the mouth like a dog, and drowning in moans of agony" (257). He feels, "in the midst of the darkness, that they were throwing him from the top of a tower into a bottomless pit" (257). Clearly, García Márquez in this chapter links overconsumption with transmutation, the act of extravagant waste making Aureliano Segundo unstuck evolutionarily as a liminal grotesque. Gluttony and waste distort Raymond L. Williams's venerated *hombre-hipoteca* (tortoise-man) "in which the human lifeworld and the lifeworld of nature are assimilated" (73). Providence *is* the fertile land in *One Hundred Years of Solitude*—its gifts miraculous—but the ruinous stewardship of Aureliano Segundo and his brood leads to the town's perdition. Either empathize with other life-forms, the novel suggests, or become the very beast you exploit.

Birds, insects, and other wildlife leave curious clues as to the greater environmental message of *One Hundred Years of Solitude.* Vultures that seek to pluck out the eyes of Aureliano Segundo's guests later descend to consume the corpse of Aureliano's father, Colonel Aureliano Buendía; these birds at once return human bodies to the food web and pick away the destructive legacies of both Aurelianos. Proliferations of yellow butterflies follow Mauricio Babilonia as he courts Meme, signifying the beneficence of their relationship. Unsurprisingly, it is the coldblooded Fernanda who both exterminates the butterflies with an "insecticide bomb" and has Mauricio shot as a chicken thief. Moreover, Pilar Ternera's "zoological brothel" conjoins mulatto prostitutes with free-range bitterns, "herons of different colors, crocodiles as fat as pigs, snakes with twelve rattles, and a turtle with a gilded shell who dove in a small artificial ocean" (*OHYS* 394). In this place of primordial bestiality where women know "ways of love that man had left behind forgotten in the earthly paradise" (394), Aureliano (son of Meme) is advised to have sex with his aunt/sister, Amaranta Úrsula. Again, transgression of the incest taboo parallels animal captivity, the trafficking of women, and aberrations of ecological habitat in a recurring genetic feedback loop to fetishization and putrefaction. These passages suggest that in Macondo's bodily relations what is called for is neither the pious rigidity of Fernanda nor the decadent excesses of Aureliano Segundo, but pleasures drawn from designs found within Colombia's own ecological systems and habitat.

Remedios the Beauty

In the liminal phase, human bodies in Macondo become chimeric, grotesque, or destructive in their irresistibility. The marriage of cousins José Arcadio Buendía and Úrsula is overshadowed by a recent ancestor born of incest who "went through life wearing loose, baggy trousers" because "he had grown up with a cartilaginous tail in the shape of a corkscrew with a small tuft of hair on the tip" (20). This porcine relation, legend has it, bled to death after having his tail chopped off because he was a virgin. After José Arcadio Buendía and Úrsula consummate their marriage, however, son José Arcadio does not have a protruding pig's tail but is described as having a penis of "disproportionate size" and being "so well-equipped for life that he seemed abnormal," causing Úrsula to relive "her newlywed terror" (25) of birth defects. Years later, little Aureliano (son of Meme) also has an "impressive sex organ that was like a turkey's wattles, as if he were not a human child but the encyclopedia definition of a cannibal" (294). Colossally distended penises in this novel effectively attract other Buendías, but the forbidden ecstasy brought about by intercourse between and among family members drawn to monstrous genitalia invariably brings the torrential flood that destroys the entire town. Remedios the Beauty endures the burden of irresistible attraction as well, but with much different results. Most of the men who have the "unfortunate privilege" (196) of seeing Remedios the Beauty "never recovered their peaceful habits of sleep" (195), and a number are even killed as a result of her crushing attractiveness. Her "suffocating odor" (233) also causes anxiety for men who fail to understand that she does "not give off a breath of love but a fatal emanation" (233). Significant is the language of toxicity and viral infection to describe carnal desire, a topic García Márquez returns to in *Love in the Time of Cholera* (1988); Remedios is described as poisonous to others but is herself "safe from any contagion" (197).

Even more telling for ecocriticism is Remedios's miraculous ascent. The astonished Buendía women are filled with shock and envy as they watch Remedios the Beauty rise "in the midst of the flapping sheets that rose up with her, abandoning with her the environment of beetles and dahlias and passing through the air with her" (236). Though José Arcadio and Aureliano are ultimately blighted in liminality, nature venerates Remedios. Why would García Márquez do this? In limbo, the novel suggests, Latin America is a place with endless boundaries yet is framed on all sides by well-defined parameters. It becomes a mirage to locals who have forsaken their regional vision in the push-and-pull of economic spectacle instigated in part by foreign opportunists who see nothing in Macondo but easy money. In this new world one can for a time ignore the limits set by nature and find overwhelming gratification, but take it too far and the results for family and community will be poison, contagion, and ultimately the birth of monsters. García Márquez's novel bemoans a century of blindness to bounds etched by American bioregions, ideological myopia, and the bedazzlement of wealth. In this unbalanced state, the Buendías begin to see the natural world as a saccharine palace akin to Willy Wonka's chocolate factory where everything can, for a time, be grabbed and consumed. Bell-Villada makes the point that "as Macondo becomes prosperous and frivolous and forgets its egalitarian and heroic past, it lays itself open to domination and destruction by outsiders—and, moreover, that solitude and lack of true solidarity are among the reasons for its eventual ruin" (*García* 89). But Remedios the Beauty offers an alternative trajectory for the liminal body, an ascendance and enchantment that are possible when in simplicity one is able to live *inside* the American mirage of limitlessness. Because the wind removes Remedios the Beauty before it destroys Macondo, she serves as one signifier of ecological *com-*

munitas, not simply as transcendence from earth but as an unlikely visionary for Latin America's environmental deliverance.

Banana Plague

The Buendías are largely responsible for the modernization of Macondo and, inadvertently, the terrors of Mr. Herbert and his banana company. As the town becomes "swamped in miraculous prosperity" (*OHYS* 193), the clear river's "prehistoric stones" are "pulverized by the frantic hammers of José Arcadio Segundo" (193), as he has "set about the awesome task of breaking stones, digging canals, clearing away rapids, and even harnessing waterfalls" (193). Though he is able to get only one log vessel filled with garish matrons through his man-made channel, nephew Aureliano Triste is much more successful in his quest "not only for the modernization of his business but to link the town with the rest of the world" (221). Aureliano Triste's machine in the jungle, his "innocent yellow train" (222), brings with it electricity, movies, French musicians, the phonograph, telephones, speculators, and offshore investors. In "permanent alternation between excitement and disappointment" (224), locals find that the town's guests seem "like people out of a circus" (224-25). Thus, for García Márquez's novel, global trade born of the railroad system becomes a furtherance of gypsy carnival marked by the selfsame costermongerism, spectacle, and gimmickry. As Conniff puts it, "the chicanery of the gypsies will only be displaced by more sophisticated and more determined exploitation" (142).

But García Márquez never gets too sentimental over Macondo's disquieting advances, nor does he spurn desires for a prosperous and modern Colombia. The novel does, however, highlight the more carnivalesque aspects of commercial development to reproach Macondo's reckless, war-hungry, profligate, and pleasure-crazed approach to the land in its haste for progress. And nowhere is García Márquez's critique more pointed than in depictions of "the banana plague" (*OHYS* 229), the novel's microcosm of political and economic practices adopted by US corporations such as the United Fruit Company in Latin America during the twentieth century. Well documented in García Márquez scholarship, Macondo serves as a primer for the habitat destruction, subjugation of native populations, resource depletion, political corruption, murder, and eventual abandonment that historically typified large-scale banana-growing practices in Central and South America.[2] The disaster begins in Macondo when Mr. Herbert, a "chubby and smiling" US businessman, devours handfuls of bananas at the Buendía table while scrutinizing a single fruit "meticulously, dissecting it with a special scalpel, weighing the pieces on a pharmacist's scale, and calculating its breadth with a gunsmith's calipers" (225). Bell-Villada finds a "marvelous political satire of Yankee technology and its more grotesque gigantisms in the elaborate hardware applied by Mr. Herbert to a harmless banana" (*García* 118), but the satire grows dark as Mr. Brown and other banana company executives move to Macondo, fence themselves in affluent gated communities, replace the policemen with "hired assassins with machetes" (*OHYS* 237), and—in a passage based on the 1928 "bloodbath" in Ciénaga, Colombia—gun down townspeople in the streets.[3] Macondo without warning becomes boomtown and banana republic, crowded once more within a festival atmosphere of "well-lit stores with products from abroad" that displace the "old bazaars with their bright colors," as well as "gaming tables, shooting galleries [in] the alley where the future was guessed and dreams interpreted" (227). The region becomes barely recognizable to locals who understand far more than their feckless new neighbors that they have usurped "means that had been reserved for Divine Providence in former times . . . changed the patterns of the rains, accelerated the cycle of harvests, and moved the river from where it had always been and put it with its white stones and icy currents on the other side of town, behind the cemetery" (227). Macondo's rainfall and agricultural cycles have apparently been altered by agribusiness practices such as crop monoculture, the digging of channels to divert river water, and arguably even cloud seeding. These methods turn ecosystems into zombiescapes that mirror the increasingly monstrous Buendía bodies.

Historically, it was depleted topsoil that prompted corporations such as the UFC to abandon Central and South American harvesting regions—and the Great Depression had much to do with the company's large-scale retreat from Colombia—but in *One Hundred Years of Solitude* the banana company is actually forced from Macondo by human-induced climate change.[4] In "The Endless Rains of Death and Desolation in García Márquez's Short Stories," Clementina R. Adams links weather conditions to a "quasi-autonomous soul" (70) that directs rains and temperature, and I believe this phantom presence can also be found in *One Hundred Years of Solitude*.[5] After Mr. Brown makes the pronouncement that the company will cease all activities until the rain stops (*OHYS* 309), Macondo is inundated with constant torrents and flooding for nearly five years! The "sky crumbled into a set of destructive storms and out of the north came hurricanes that scattered roofs about and knocked down walls and uprooted every last plant of the banana groves" (315); thus, untimely storms punish Mr. Brown and his corporation to reverse the Macondo region's advances. Regina Janes argues that the "company brings the banana plague, but that plague is prosperity and connectedness, the raft and the train, and when it goes, prosperity abandons the town, leaving a wreck behind" ("Revisiting" 467). But an ecocritical reading of Macondo's plague years suggests that the town's loss will also bring unexpected opportunities for renewal. After both the rain and the novel's ultimate storm, the "enchanted region explored by José Arcadio Buendía in the days of the founding, where later on the banana plantations flourished, was a bog of rotting roots, on the horizon of which one could manage to see the silent foam of the sea" (*OHYS* 331). From the perspective of the Faulknerian Buendías and others who have lost their fortunes in the deluge, Macondo is most assuredly in ruins. But as depicted here, the rain also marks a joyous tragedy. The rotting bog with a view to the sea is again at the germinal stage of a slow return to "enchanted" conditions from which life can begin anew.

By revealing new flowers in Macondo's ruins, this novel asks readers not to jump to apocalyptic conclusions but to seek out recessionary joys and even beauty and purpose in economic decline. During the rains the "driest of machines would have flowers popping out of their gears if they were not oiled every three days" (315), and after the "prophetic wind" the "only human trace left by that voracious blast was a glove belonging to Patricia Brown in an automobile smothered in wild pansies" (331). Because plant and animal species in this book offer missives as liminal creatures, the recurring image of flowers bursting from inert machines signifies the Macondo bioregion's reanimation in the wake of boomtown destruction. The "banana company had left," García Márquez writes, and "Macondo finally had peace after many years" (384): "The survivors of the catastrophe, the same ones who had been living in Macondo before it had been struck by the banana company hurricane, were sitting in the middle of the street enjoying their first sunshine. They still had the green of the algae on their skin and the musty smell of a corner that had been stamped on them by the rain, but in their hearts they seemed happy to have recovered the town in which they had been born" (331). Significant here is the language of recovery to describe the devastation of a town, the paradox of rejuvenation through ruin key to seeing around the novel's apocalyptic denouement. Locals who have ridden out Colombian storms both political and climatic have also become threshold beings with traits of both human and plant life . . . a peculiar but healthy adaptation. And whether or not the novel actually longs for ruins, the boomtown's collapse certainly becomes the precipitating moment wherein humans and the landscape imaginatively move beyond liminality and find safe passage from Latin America's troubled history, lingering nostalgia, and foolish relatives.

House of Horrors

In this light, the ever-changing condition of the Buendía home provides a useful case study in resource management, as Macondo's bioregion truly becomes reflected in the "order of the house" (Tittler 12).

Úrsula, the family's bedrock, designs a family homestead complete with gardens, a granary, a "large stable, a fenced-in chicken yard, a shed for the milk cows, and an aviary open to the four winds so that wandering birds could roost there at their pleasure" (*OHYS* 54); after Colonel Aureliano Buendía's convalescence, it is Úrsula who restores the garden and opens windows so that the "dazzling light of summer would penetrate even into the bedrooms" (180). To protect the "foundations of the house," the aged matriarch keeps at bay termites and the "enormous red ants that had prospered during the deluge" (334); in so doing, she maintains a symbolic balance between Macondo and the surrounding ecosystem. Like Remedios the Beauty, Úrsula differs from her various offspring and relatives because she lives within limits inside a mirage of limitlessness. But unlike Fernanda who keeps doors and windows shut—a fruitless struggle for purity and containment—Úrsula resists the excesses of both repression and hedonism that lead to Macondo's undoing. Úrsula's prolonged death therefore marks the final stage of Macondo's threshold experience. With her stewardship and vision lost, there emerges a "certain confusion in nature: the roses smelled like goose foot [and] a pod of chickpeas fell down and the beans lay on the ground in a perfect geometrical pattern in the shape of a starfish" (342). Thousands of birds die en masse, and the house plunges "into a crisis of senility"; with preternatural speed, a "soft moss grew up the walls" and "weeds broke through the cement of the porch, breaking it like glass" (358). Unable to "halt the challenges of nature" after Úrsula dies, Santa Sofía de la Piedad finds that the "ants had left the undermined foundations, crossed the garden, climbed up the railing, where the begonias had taken on an earthen color, and had penetrated into the heart of the house" (358). Nature, we see, not only abhors a vacuum but also will repossess a vacuous home.

Plants, animals, wind, and rain work collectively to remove the Buendía house from the earth because, from the perspective of Macondo's bioregion, the last one hundred years just didn't pan out. And from the point of view of García Márquez—a brilliant young man who watched his own philandering father hatch countless harebrained schemes, as well as what he saw as a clown show of Colombian political leaders who spiraled in pointless cycles of violence and waste—perhaps the ecological theater offered more compelling models for a "sweeping utopia of life" (García Márquez, "Nobel Lecture") than the shared wisdom of man. Maybe it was simply impossible at that time for García Márquez to see a political path to the world he dreamed of coming from his own historical circumstances. To experience *One Hundred Years of Solitude* is to "feel all the writer's accumulated frustration, and scorn, and anger at a country which endlessly consumed its own children and seemed as though it would never, ever change" (Martin 246). Perhaps at the time García Márquez felt that only a painful rite might bring the reanimation of his Colombian earth, one that would finally turn its house of horrors upside down.

Though Amaranta Úrsula returns generations later to restore the house, her attempts prove futile because she has in effect become a nonindigenous species. Like the birds she ships from the Canary Islands and Madeira (Fortunate Isles), she is no longer suited to inhabit Macondo. Seized by an overwhelming nostalgia, Amaranta Úrsula releases the canaries, "and no sooner did they feel themselves free than they fled the town" (*OHYS* 379). Despite the "artificial nests built of esparto grass in the almond trees and the birdseed strewn about the roofs . . . they would take flight on their first attempt and make a turn in the sky, just in the time needed to find the direction to the Fortunate Isles" (379). In this phantom zone, non-native birds in their hasty retreat caution Amaranta Úrsula to flee Macondo as well. Though she cannot float away like Remedios the Beauty, she might still fly to the Fortunate Isles with Gaston. She instead gives birth to the long-awaited "mythological animal," the deformed child of incest that becomes key to decoding the parchments of Melquíades. As he looks for his misplaced pig-tailed newborn, Aureliano the last—in the portentous final moments of his own life—admires the "persistence of the spiderwebs on the dead rosebushes, the perseverance of the rye grass, the patience of the air in the radiant February dawn." This is, of course, when he sees his child, a "dry and bloated bag of skin that all the ants in the world were dragging toward the holes along the stone path in the garden" (414). Aureliano at this instant recovers the biocentric vision lost by José Arcadio Buendía a long century ago; he perceives that despite all his family's undoing in Macondo that spiders persist, grasses persevere, and the dawn still radiates life. The world will heal, and future generations will reflect on the rusted car alongside the armor and the galleon, all monuments to the failures of conquest. "Liminality," Turner offers, "may be partly described as a stage of reflection" (*Forest* 105), and Aureliano has this fleeting moment to reflect on biodiversity's monstrous beauty and powers of renewal. Importantly, this revelation comes at dawn. "Condemned" Macondo is not rendered extinct so that *nothing* will take its place. The biosphere leaves no place for nothing.

The Opposite Utopia

At the moment his newborn son is pulled into the ground by ants, Aureliano is finally able to decrypt the parchments found "intact among the prehistoric plants and steaming puddles and luminous insects that had removed all trace of man's passage on earth from the room" (*OHYS* 415). Melquíades's room is as close to Eden as contemporary readers get in the second half of *One Hundred Years of Solitude*, and it too is lost in the storm. The wind that rises begins "warm, incipient, full of voices from the past, the murmurs of ancient geraniums, sighs of disenchantment that preceded the most tenacious nostalgia" (416); it's a grave oversight to assume that the voices heard while Aureliano is reading the parchment are human voices. The geraniums, however, do speak. And their "disenchantment" with Macondo is carried by a wind of "cyclonic strength" that destroys the Buendía house, uprooting its very foundations (416). The five-year rain makes Macondo pause, its effects curative for the town because it drives back the banana company just as the "biblical hurricane" (416) at the novel's end intervenes to give Macondo a second chance to bloom.

Cognitive dissonance brought about by the artist's imaginings of what is and what might yet be produces in *One Hundred Years of Solitude* both monsters and angels, beings that in their liminality push the reader to conceive Latin America from an elevated, mutualistic perspective. As García Márquez declared in 1982 when he accepted the Nobel Prize in Literature:

> On a day like today, my master William Faulkner said, "I decline to accept the end of man." I would fall unworthy of standing in this place that was his, if I were not fully aware that the colossal tragedy he refused to recognize thirty-two years ago is now, for the first time since the beginning of humanity, nothing more than a simple scientific possibility. Faced with this awesome reality that must have seemed a mere utopia through all of human time, we, the inventors of tales, who will believe anything, feel entitled to believe that it is not yet too late to engage in the creation of the opposite utopia. A new and sweeping utopia of life, where no one will be able to decide for others how they die, where love will prove true and happiness be possible, and where the races condemned to one hundred years of solitude will have, at last and forever, a second opportunity on earth. (García Márquez, "Nobel Lecture")

It's conventional wisdom that the last line of the speech is a revision of the final passage of *One Hundred Years of Solitude*, which reads: "[F]or it was foreseen that the city of mirrors (or mirages) would be wiped out by the wind and exiled from the memory of men at the precise moment when Aureliano Babilonia would finish deciphering the parchments, and that everything written on them was unrepeatable since time immemorial and forever more, because races condemned to one hundred years of solitude did not have a second opportunity on earth" (416–17). In liminality, I believe, it becomes possible for the "opposite utopia" that García Márquez speaks of in his Nobel speech—his far-reaching and hopeful vision—to be found right there in the final passage of *One Hundred Years of Solitude.* As Janes pronounces in *Gabriel García Márquez: Revolutions in Wonderland* (1981), it is the "mind's capacity for imagining what does not exist and its dissatisfaction with what does that are finally the only means by which the world is ever transformed" (69). Dissonance created by the destruction of Macondo creates an imaginative longing that compels the reader to conceptually and materially begin again. Amid ruins the opposite utopia appears.

In *Writing the Apocalypse,* Lois Parkinson Zamora describes Macondo as "cyclical in the Spenglerian sense that the town participates in growth, maturity, decline, death, and rebirth. This is certainly so in the course of Macondo's 100-year history, both those 100 years do come to an end, and rebirth ultimately fails to occur" (27). But on the following page she writes that the "events that destroy Macondo—the oppression of the banana company, the strike and massacre of the banana company workers, the ensuing flood—lead to the inevitable moment when Macondo will be blown away, and the tropics will reclaim its territory" (28). But how can "rebirth" fail to occur if the "tropics will reclaim its territory"? Rebirth is found in bioreclamation, and García Márquez's Nobel speech confirms his belief that Macondo and its real-life Latin American counterparts will in all likelihood have a better chance to thrive when released from the socioeconomic bonds created by the banana company, the leftist rebels, the conservative party, and the generations of misguided opportunists found in the novel. Zamora writes that in "García Márquez's tropics, temporal resolution, even cataclysmic resolution, comes to seem welcome. In accordance with apocalyptic convention, all that can be anticipated is the end of time itself" (30). But, as we who live in the twenty-first century are often reminded, time doesn't just *end* when large-scale environmental catastrophes strike. In works of magical realism such as *One Hundred Years of Solitude* and Yamashita's *Tropic of Orange,* time reshapes and redirects.[6] Raymond L. Williams points out that *One Hundred Years of Solitude* "claims as its hermeneutic horizon the finite environment the reader occupies thanks not just to culturally coded determinants but also to natural determinants that antedate these, and will outlast them" (75). And in the case of *Tropic of Orange,* it is precisely a hermeneutics of "natural determinants" such as fruit that yields the novel's more potent lessons.

From UFC to NAFTA

Yamashita's orange, like García Márquez's metonymic banana, propels human figures in at-risk ecosystems to catastrophe and beyond. Near Mazatlán, young mother Rafaela Cortes fixates on an "aberrant orange" in the backyard orchard of L.A. reporter Gabriel Balboa. It is described as an "orange that should not have been" (Yamashita 11) because it has bloomed prematurely due to erratic changes in climate. This anomalous fruit is also magically attached to the Tropic of Cancer, and Rafaela can see a thin latitudinal line running east to west through the orange and along Gabriel's orchard. When the orange falls from the tree, the taut line moves as well, pulling with it the unfixed geography and climate of Mexico. In its migration northward to Los Angeles, the orange pushes both garden and city into an increasingly liminal state, "unsettling all rules of space and time" (Lee 506), and prompting among other things a meditation on NAFTA that advances García Márquez's critique of syndicates such as the United Fruit Company (now Chiquita Brands International). The orange makes the "familiar landscape of Los Angeles and the whole of the southwest region down to the Tropic of Cancer move, condense, and rearrange itself in a dramatic literalization of geographical and cultural deterritorialization" (Song 571). Migrating toward the United States, the orange "marks an intersection of multiple global influences in the forms of transcontinental trade and colonialism" (Gamber 141), networks interconnected within a layered, porous, and increasingly globalized L.A.

Like José Arcadio Buendía, Gabriel in *Tropic of Orange* unsettles his household because he has lost touch with the local. Rather than filling his second home with costly contraptions, however, Gabriel plants a variety of "exotic northern trees" (Yamashita 11) and nonindigenous plants in a vexed orchard that is diverse but incoherent. Gabriel's garden has become a place, to quote Elisabeth Mermann-Jozwiak, that "complicates and destabilizes the concept of 'setting / location' by interweaving with it the notion of travel, tracing the roots and migratory / trade routes that produce a view of the city [garden] as a site of convergence for people [life-forms] from around the globe and a nexus that links heterogeneous spaces" (Mermann-Jozwiak 2). Gabriel's phantom garden, certainly a "nexus that links heterogeneous spaces," also serves as blueprint for a more bioregional and sustainable Los Angeles. Reminiscent of Úrsula in *One Hundred Years of Solitude,* Rafaela keeps up the Balboa household by sweeping away the daily "pile of assorted insects and tiny animals" (Yamashita 3); on the property she plants local "cactus and sunflowers, chiles and corn, kitchen and medicinal herbs" (10). By moving Rafaela's methods along with Gabriel's backyard to the City of Angels, *Tropic of Orange* offers sustainable agriculture as key to reterritorializing urban Los Angeles and thwarting the homogenizing forces embodied in the monstrous villain SUPERNAFTA.

Elasticity

The orange, its tangled line, and Rafaela's son Sol are transported across the Mexico-US border by a fantastic Márquezian personage named

Arcangel, a five-hundred-year-old performance artist who has wings that "didn't seem fake, weren't strapped on or glued to his back, but were growing there" (48); he is also described as having a "body-tree," the "beauty of an ancient body, a gnarled and twisted tree, tortured and serene, wise and innocent all at once" (47). Arcangel mutates morphologically to display attributes of both animal and plant life, which signifies his status as ecological limen; as threshold figure he is also a migrant on a journey national and bioregional borders. Arcangel the "[u]r-trickster, shape shifter, shaman, prophet, and superman," demonstrates in his movements "the elasticity of space" (Mermann-Jozwiak 16) as well as the mutability of species. In his journey north Arcangel occasionally becomes El Gran Mojado, the famous masked Mexican wrestler who is scheduled to stage a grudge match in the United States against his colossal archenemy, a fighter with a flaming head who dons a "titanium body suit" (Yamashita 261) and has missiles for fingers: the mighty SUPERNAFTA. South of the border, Arcangel is the only person who eats *nopales* at the Cantina de Miseria y Hambre, while "all the hungry and miserable people in the cantina" sit eating "hamburgers, Fritos, catsup, and drinking American beers" (131). While it is true that Arcangel's threshold experience signifies a "provocative deconstruction of geopolitical boundaries" (Mermann-Jozwiak 16), his performative place-shifting and topographical stretching exist to inspire local community building and enlightened urban planning.

Another figure in L.A. limbo who seeks to reawaken the city's ecological imagination is Manzanar Murakami, the Japanese American "conductor" who stands on overpasses and stages great symphonies to the sounds of L.A. traffic. Using "metaphors of a living body to depict the freeway" (R. Adams 248–49), Manzanar sees the elaborate interstate system at times as an animal body and at others a "great root system, an organic living entity" (Yamashita 37). Critic Sue-Im Lee explains that Manzanar "sees the artificial construct in the same realm as the elemental structures of nature, and through the language of elemental organism, describes the interconnected nature of urban existence" (515). But despite his provocative street performances, Manzanar recognizes that most Angelinos will

> never bother to notice the prehistoric grid of plant and fauna and human behavior, nor the historic grid of land usage and property, the great overlays of transport—sidewalks, bicycle paths, roads, freeways, systems of transit both ground and air, a thousand natural and man-made divisions, variations both dynamic and stagnant, patterns and connections by every conceivable definition from the distribution of wealth to race, from patterns of climate to the curious blueprint of the skies. (Yamashita 57)

From Manzanar's multidimensional vision—one that he invites the entire city to embrace—the freeway itself becomes part of an intricate crossbred organism that creates an "uncanny sense of the elasticity of the moment, of time and space" (123). As catalyst for this phantasmic urbanity, Manzanar oversees protuberances and breakdowns along the global transit system to reinvigorate the freeway as a liminal zone with long-forgotten ecological potential.

When a colossal truck crash causes a major traffic jam, hundreds of people from the roadside emerge to occupy the freeway. The dispossessed and homeless who inhabit the "dense hidden community living on the no-man's-land of public property" (120) co-opt concretized structures in creative actions, to include using stalled cars as homes. Sarah D. Wald explains that through Manzanar, "Yamashita focuses on the possibility of reclaiming the freeway as an abstract space of capital for the living communities of displaced and dispossessed peoples" (87). This reclamation project also transforms the relationship between people and their impromptu gardens, which makes the freeway suddenly a vehicle for the values of wise use. Repurposed automobiles become not only houses but also phone booths, civic centers, and stores as the street scene becomes increasingly carnivalesque; the dispossessed enact "one of those happy riots" (Yamashita 122) that later merges on the freeway with Arcangel's "motley parade" (238) of immigrants. Through Manzanar, the reader experiences a perfect example of an ecological void—the concrete interstate system—as a place of promise. In liminality, this cognitively remapped thoroughfare reverses the flow of energies leading to social inequality, a greater carbon footprint, and dependency on fossil fuels. Because of the catastrophic automobile crash and the United States' collision course with the Tropic of Cancer, the dispossessed become "planners designing a new mixed-use suburban development" (Song 570), to include a recycling program, a waste management system, and even public showers: every "morning at 3:00 a.m., the landscaping sprinkler system goes on like clockwork. Mamas all run out with their kids at the break of dawn to take advantage of the shower" (Yamashita 218). Yamashita also adds local food production to this equation by describing how one neighbor "got a tomato plant growing in the dirt coming up through the concrete. 'You see here, these blossoms? And there's baby tomatoes. Call it urban gardening. We gonna be feeding ourselves, don't you worry'" (217). Buzzworm the enigmatic street activist also recognizes the value and import of the freeway's occupation, because people are "finally getting out, close to the ground, seeing the city like he did" (219). As Min Hyoung Song shows, Yamashita's fiction "provides an active commentary on a world full-to-bursting with dreamlike tension between culture and nature, between human activities and the physical world, between global inequality and catastrophes that await to be visited on everyone" (570-71). In *Tropic of Orange,* all of these tensions come to a head on the L.A. freeway, and this leaves readers with not only catastrophe—the homeless people are forcibly removed—but also a profound yearning for L.A. to embrace spatial reanimation and environmental justice as foundations for food production and urban planning.

Shifting City

Rafaela also gets pulled into the phantom zone on her journey to Los Angeles and becomes both migrant and shape-shifter. Realizing that Doña Maria's son Hernando is an organ trafficker who is trying to abduct two-year-old Sol to harvest a kidney, Rafaela must leave her son (and the orange) with Arcangel, who just so happens to be going north as well. Kidnapped and assaulted by Hernando, the "villain of the Jaguar" (Yamashita 185), Rafaela twists "her body into a muscular serpent" and thrashes at him with "vicious fangs—ripping his ears, gouging his neck, drawing blood" (220). Having transformed from a Jag-driving hood literally into a big cat, the villain pounces, ripping "into the armored scales of her tensile body" (220); as mortal enemies, Rafaela and Hernando begin their "horrific dance with death, gutting and searing the tissue of their existence, copulating in rage, destroying and creating at once—the apocalyptic fulfillment of a prophecy—blood and semen commingling among shredded serpent and feline remains" (221).[7] In the morning Rafaela is badly hurt but comes to realize that, perchance, she has eaten both Hernando and his car! Rafaela the prophetic she-serpent has triumphed by containing Yamashita's agent of Pan American economic exploitation, the villainous broker of transplanted fruits and organs. Skillfully, Márquezian tropes of bestiality, the grotesque, and hyperbolic consumption are used in this passage of *Tropic of Orange* to expose the dark underbelly of free trade.

Rafaela's final act in this novel is to cut the orange—severing with it the Tropic of Cancer—and then feed the fruit to the ailing Arcangel. This moment of cartographic deconstruction and ritual healing becomes an invitation for readers to disavow the imaginary boundaries that separate nation, race, and class and instead embrace fruitful bioregional urban communities as they emerge and merge throughout the Americas. This moment also challenges Angelinos on every side of the border to imaginatively and materially reanimate urban zombiescapes that "regenerate repeatedly under pressures of forces both local and global" (Chuh 621). Using "predominant themes of self-regeneration, transformation and re-cycling" (Tekdemir 50), Yamashita maps out a truly transnational metropolis for the sake of promoting social mobility, sustainable living, and bioregional trade. In the pages of *Tropic of Orange,* Los Angeles becomes a "nodal point where globalization threatens to erupt into environmental and human catastrophe, but also where people find themselves creating unlikely coalitions that might work to remedy these problems" (R. Adams 252). With the defeat of SUPERNAFTA, Rafaela and her family will find coalitions in the city of Los Angeles and *communitas* in one another. Rafaela's husband Bobby who is still attached to the lines separating the tropics, arms outstretched, must let go—let the "lines slither around his wrists, past his palms, through his fingers" (Yamashita 268)—to at last embrace his family and the shifting city that enfolds them. Here, Yamashita takes it upon herself to resolve the central problem left at the end of *One Hundred Years of Solitude* by making both novels' most enduring emblem of *communitas*—the family—triumphant in the face of precipitous change.

2
Eerie Cartographies in Thomas Pynchon's *Mason & Dixon* and Don DeLillo's *Underworld*

GPS satellites have orbited the globe since the Department of Defense launched its first NAVSTAR Global Positioning System in 1978. Now there are two doxen GPS satellites orbiting the planet, and anyone with a forty-dollar receiver can pinpoint his or her location pretty much anywhere on earth. With Google Maps it's a piece of cake to navigate the entire Western Hemisphere, the best routes from Prudhoe Bay to Ushuaia instantly available for anyone with Internet access. GPS, Google Maps, and Google Earth are certainly of great benefit to environmental organizations, because they can do such things as collect data on species migrations, chart areas damaged by drought or flood over time, and monitor toxic sites. But the ability to tread on un-Googled ground is all but impossible now, the total capture of the earth's surface virtually complete by the mind in the cloud. How do these instruments change the way we understand and experience actual borders, boundaries, and bioregions? How does the human brain compute the unnamed regions on our maps, those marginal expanses on screen or page that lack contour and color? These are the strange coordinates where Thomas Pynchon and Don DeLillo dwell in *Mason & Dixon* (1997) and *Underworld* (1997), places where government-commissioned practitioners of science—surveyors, rocket scientists, and waste managers—can only partially identify the spaces they map, calculate, and name. Disquieting geographies emerge from these cognitive rifts to become unclassified, unseen, and double; as Pynchon's "blank space on the Map" (*MD* 336) or DeLillo's "white space on the map" (DeLillo 451), liminal coordinates defy national will and become instead poltergeists of American fear. The Mason-Dixon Line in Pynchon's novel becomes a catalyzing force that conjures zombiescapes and phantom zones, and correspondingly in DeLillo's novel the A-bomb generates both malformed bodies and militarized landscapes. The construction of borderlines in both novels produces abject and chimeric creatures that resist cartographic containment and the burden of history as they invariably turn on their creators. Employing historical figures, pastiche, and their own trademark strains of paranoia, Pynchon and DeLillo turn postmodernism against itself to chart paths to a better world.

The Line

Astronomer Charles Mason and surveyor Jeremiah Dixon trekked across the North American wilderness from 1763 to 1767 to make their mark on the New World, an ax-cut strip 233 miles, 17.48 chains long that would map out the vast influence of Penns and Calverts for years to come and also cleave the physical landscape for the sake of further progress.[1] Neither mathematician could have imagined the larger social and ecological strain the Mason-Dixon Line would cause for future generations, though entries in *The Journal of Charles Mason and Jeremiah Dixon* (1969) describe cutting their way through an overwhelming terrain of material abundance, harsh weather, and bioregional diversity that tested both colonial ideology and the most cutting-edge scientific equipment of that time. In September 1764, for example, Mason finds in Pocomoke Swamp the "greatest quantity of Timber [he] ever saw: Above the Tallest Oak, Beech, Poplar, Hickory, Holly and Fir; Towers the lofty Cedar: (without a Branch), till its ever green conical top; seems to reach the clouds: The pleasing sight of which; renewed my wishes to see Mount Lebanon" (*MD* 63); the next day's entry in the *Journal* simply reads: "Engaging ax men, providing Boards for marks, etc." (63). In these telling passages, trees immense in both size and number draw ax-wielding admirers who expose, in the felling of old-growth trees, a cultural pathology characterized by the drive to form imposing landscapes into geometric shapes to give unsettled settlers some sense of dominion. The resulting line, or "visto," brings to light the trouble with accurately calculating and mapping an ever-changing ecological being that evades stasis and containment, while the paradox of Enlightenment order and proportion born of ecological ruin makes the very concept of "border" or "boundary" an erroneous descriptor. Paranormal creatures emerge from such contradictory physical spaces to perturb the linearity of colonial history in this novel described as a historiographical "meditation on lines, boundaries, borders, margins, and their consequences" (Harris 207).

Geodetic oddities proliferate in Pynchon's novel to raise a proper carnival of New World freaks and phantasms along the shared borders of Delaware, Maryland, Pennsylvania, and Virginia. Like *Gravity's Rainbow* (1973), this monster of a novel transits "different ontological levels that, by transgressing their boundaries, produce a continual impression of instability and uncertainty in the reader that tries to apply western logic to the act of reading" (Collado-Rodriguez 77). Liminal monsters and paranormal visitants haunt the Line, and from its eerie fault come weird, gigantic, alien, shadowy, and fetishized lands measured and misinterpreted by eighteenth-century science and pseudoscience. The chimera that emerges in wildly different forms "troubles as an active conceptual linkage between idea and matter that overturns the relations of body and ground, before and after in its power to potently reconceive groundless abstract, speculative, and fantastic ideas in the form of living matter" (Casid 63). Idea turns into matter, and body becomes ground, which frees Pynchon's hallmark entropic and uncertain stylizations to move the novel's animus beyond the needling paranoia, existential void, or imaginative fatalism of imminent empire. By giving the land agency and interrogating geodetic surveying techniques in the bewildering textual wild, *Mason & Dixon* produces for Pynchon's reader a characteristic giddiness and mystical flux that reveals, perhaps uncharacteristically, the presence and purpose of environmental advocacy. Moreover, Pynchon's reconceptualization of the celebrated surveyors for a contemporary audience challenges readers to look to America's colonial past for strains of opposition that inform policy and behavior in the twenty-first century.

Elizabeth Jane Wall Hinds explains that in *Mason & Dixon* the "natural world, and with it, the physics on which nature depends "exists in" a kind of boundary state wherein categories of 'kind' are likely to cross over—from animal to human or human to vegetable or animal to machine" (Hinds, "Introduction" 4). But such "border phenomena" (Hinds, "Animal" 181) don't lead inescapably to the "spatial entropy" (Hinds, "Introduction" 4) one might expect from the author of *V* and *The Crying of Lot 49.* Instead, totemic landscapes emerge from border phenomena like the Great Serpent Mound found near Brush Creek Valley in Ohio[2] to signify a natural world animate and comprehensible in unlearned semiologies of landscape. Pynchon's conspiracies of nature move readers beyond the subjunctive to the liminal as a means to re-enchant contemporary readers with forgotten formations that yet exist within hallowed American grounds. In this context, Mason and Dixon embody "an eighteenth-century obsession with extremes of the natural world, the 'science' that vivifies the mechanical, the 'natural' that borders on and intersects with the supernatural" (6). Pynchon's vivification of monstrous bioregions keeps alive the contention even now, over two hundred years after Mason and Dixon's journey, that the United States has not reached the end of the line, that there's still a chance to become a nation that has the courage to face our current challenges by taking such steps as doubling down with investments in alternative energy and embracing the Paris climate accord. Reading *Mason & Dixon* biocentrically also frees readers to see natural flora and fauna as beings analogous to hybrids or cyborgs, but within an evolutionary continuum that still leaves time. Approaching the novel's plants, animals, and bioregions as liminal beings uncovers a Pynchonian paradigm that advances the postcolonial Americas from impending crisis to ecological *communitas*.

Victor Turner explains that liminal bodies elude classification and are "neither here nor there; they are betwixt and between the positions assigned and arrayed by law, custom, convention, and ceremonial" (*Ritual* 95). Monsters in *Mason & Dixon* such as golems, dragons, and werebeavers—as well as gigantic vegetable gardens and the infamous "Delaware Triangle"—characterize imperiled natural environments in the face of colonial seizure and scientific classification. If "liminality is regarded as a time and place of withdrawal from normal modes of social action," Turner explains, "it can be seen as potentially a period of scrutinization of the central values and axioms of the culture in which it occurs" (167). Thus, when the surveyors create an eight-yard divide between Pennsylvania and Maryland, they open the forest floor to both biotic growth and political reform.

Golem

Paranormal entities expose cryptic designs in *Mason & Dixon* because Pynchon's entropic stylizations, conspiratorial tenor, absurd humor, and lowbrow twentieth-century cultural references lead here not to gleeful literary heat death but to a surprisingly cogent call to action regarding land use. Here the author uses his hypermodern bag of tricks to meditate on the narcissistic surveying strategies imposed upon the natural world within irresolute British colonies. There is a correlation between the cutting of old-growth trees and creatures like Pynchon's Golem, between the charting of emerging empire and corporeal defilement on a continental scale. The Golem is invisible when in motion, a property "shar'd with this whole accursed Continent" (*MD* 486), but when "it [becomes] necessary to our Souls that it come to rest," Golem and landscape alike are "self-reveal'd" (486). Derived from Jewish legend, Pynchon's Golem is described as a misshapen humanoid avenger "made of Water and Earth,—Clay, that is, and Minerals" (685). In Pynchon's cosmology both Golem and the soil it protects can be seen and understood only when human culture has the spiritual capacity to allow "rest" or liberty from the surveyors' instruments.

Pynchon's American Golem, "created by an Indian tribe widely suppos'd to be one of the famous Lost Tribes of Israel," has been sent "headlong into the Forest" (485); this monster is bound to a telluric, nonhuman divinity that survives "deluded . . . Inhabitants" of the New World who "feed the Metropolis, open new roads to it, [and] fight in its behalf" (488). Because the Golem "takes a dim view of Oppression, and is ever available to exert itself to the Contrary" (490), it has spurned British governance and now serves as an agent of change. As the creature moves toward a village, "Bears, Bobcats, and Wolves come fleeing" (490), and "great Mud Feet are seen to stir, tall as the Eaves" (490). Mason imagines that the Golem appears "as if an Indian Mound of the West, struck by Lightning, had risen, stood, and, newly awaken'd, with the *Vis Fulgoris* surging among all its precisely fashion'd Laminae, begun, purposefully, to walk" (685). Pynchon conflates the Native American burial mound with ornate references to Mary Shelley's *Frankenstein* to describe earth that has been naturalized by invention but transmogrified to vex its purpose. As New World daemon, the Golem embodies the liminality created when "Forms of the Land, the flow of water, the occurrence of what us'd to be call'd Miracles, all are Text,—to be attended to, manipulated, read, remember'd" (487). Like DeLillo's atom bomb, Pynchon's Golem defies the textualization of natural form by becoming inconceivable to expose the scientists' "futile attempt to subordinate a world that is sublimely insubordinate" (Millard 114).

Dragons, Worms, and Ghost-Fish

Dragons concealed in Native American mounds also prove insubordinate to expansionist rhetoric, and the bioregion surrounding each creature is subsequently transformed into what William B. Millard deems "Pynchonian space." Millard argues that Pynchon's works reveal "a recurrent historical concept, which I would term 'Pynchonian space' or 'the Pynchonian moment,' whereby political, socio-economic, and intellectual vectors intersect to create a temporary realm of augmented personal autonomy, political anarchy, epistemologic uncertainty, and narrative possibilities both comic and tragic" (105–6). Pynchon's mounds, where "intellectual vectors intersect" with the paranormal, constitute part of a wider conspiracy that "may allow some resistance to . . . environmental degradation" (106). Importantly, Millard highlights a causal relationship between cutting the visto and the epistemological uncertainty of place that gives birth to dragons and other preternatural serpents. As geomancer Captain Zhang tries to convey in this oft-cited passage: "Ev'rywhere else on earth, Boundaries follow Nature,—coastlines, ridge-tops, river-banks,—so honoring the Dragon or *Shan* within, from which Land-Scape ever takes its form. To mark a right Line upon the Earth is to inflict upon the Dragon's very Flesh, a sword-slash, a long, perfect scar, impossible for any who live out here the year 'round to see as other than hateful Assault. How can it pass unanswer'd?" (*MD* 542). The Line "acts as a Conduit for what we call *Sha*," which is "Bad Energy" (542). Using the Chinese magnetic compass, or *Luo Pan*, Captain Zhang's job is to consider the feng-shui of lands cut in two. Understood as a "system of spirit influences, good and evil, which inhabit the natural features of landscapes" ("feng-shui"), feng-shui might be styled in this instance as the "union of Heaven and Earth and specifically to the electromagnetic field that holds all matter together" ("Luo Pan Chinese Compass"). Pynchon's dragons reside in earth mounds that are connected to the surrounding landscape through a combination of spiritual and electromagnetic forces; like the Golem, dragons serve as both defenders of precolonized biomes and a curse upon ecological despoilers.

The St. Helena Dragon, for example, is described by Nevil Maskelyne[3] as a being that "[r]ules this Island, whose ancient Curse and secret Name, is Disobedience" (*MD* 135). Maskelyne tells Mason that in "thoughtless Greed, within a few pitiable brief Generations, have these People devastated a Garden in which, once, anything might grow. Their Muck-heaps ev'rywhere" (135). Uninhabited until claimed in succession from 1502 onward by Portuguese, Dutch, and British invaders, St. Helena suffers "whilst the unremitting Wind carries off the last soil from the last barren Meadow" until humans who "disobey themselves into Oblivion" (135) are the "only life remaining then to the Island" (135). This aptly named dragon couples the islanders' ruinous practices toward their own garden on St. Helena with the original disobedience of the Christian tradition wherein the mythical Adam and Eve disturb the Garden of Eden by taking more than needed for the viability of their species. Significantly, this passage links the dragon's curse with two key ecological problems of the twentieth and twenty-first centuries: waste management and species extinction. We gather from this passage that the ecological injustices of the European and British islanders have conjured a paranormal visitant that will plague both land and human "into Oblivion" unless they learn to heed and respect the island's latent garden. We note again in this passage that Pynchonian space is not inevitably apocalyptic, because oblivion can be reversed through acts of remembrance. Unlike catastrophes, curses are made to be lifted through redemptive acts.

At North Mountain past the Allegheny Crest, Dixon tells Captain Zhang the legend of another dragonlike creature and in so doing lays out the core environmental logic of *Mason & Dixon*. The Lambton Worm of legend, a sharp-toothed snakelike monster, grows to colossal size after John Lambton tosses it into a well and gallops off to a crusade in Transylvania. The liminal Worm, now "so large that it may comfortably coil 'round the entire Castle" (590), has created a "Zone of emptiness" (590), a "circle of Devastation . . . pale and soil'd, which no one enters, and which the World must keep shifting for, a little at a time, as it goes on widening" (589). Upon returning to Lambton Castle, John kills the Worm in a ferocious battle but is left for generations with the curse "that no Lord of Lambton die in his bed" (594). The mistake that has brought forth the Worm, like that of the St. Helena Dragon, is another of the novel's errors in biogeography. The region surrounding Lambton Castle has been transformed into a "Zone of emptiness" or "circle of Devastation" because Lambton has taken the Worm from its natural habitat and thoughtlessly released it where it doesn't belong. Like Asian carp in the Great Lakes, the invasive or "alien" species once outside of its habitat devastates the surrounding ecosystem.[4] Here, Lambton the Crusader is blighted for being oblivious to the vulnerable domain that exists beyond the castle gates.

Eerie ghost-fish, described to Mason and Dixon as they cross the Youghiogheny River, also link human error to haunted ecologies, which are places beset by specters left by past wrongs. Described as "big as a man or Woman, pale as a floating Corpse," with "two sets of Fins each side and a Tail like a Dragon's" (660), the ghost-fish, or "Ghosters," have a curious connection in *Mason & Dixon* to Braddock's defeat in 1755, when General Edward Braddock's force of over 1,400 British soldiers was soundly defeated on the Monongahela River by roughly six hundred Indians and thirty French colonial troops. As ferryman Immanuel Ice entwines these two tales, "mist from the River halts in its Ascent, the Frogs pause between Croaks, and the peepers in mid-peep. The great black cobbles of the River-bed stir and knock no longer. The Dead are being summon'd" (659). Like Charon, who ferries travelers across the River Styx to the Underworld, Mr. Ice takes the crew to a phantom zone where "Time . . . is abolish'd" (659); he says that the Ghosters' "entire lives are engulf'd unceasingly in change. They never come to rest. They never know an Instant of Tranquility"; he questions if "this World be already their Purgatory, and they no longer classifiable as living Fish" (660). Mason and Dixon come to an important place in their journey, though neither at that time catches a glimpse of this zombie fish or its greater meaning. Pynchon exposes the eighteenth-century surveyors' incomplete understanding of this American landscape and its species so that contemporary readers might recognize and correct similar misunderstandings in our own time. The ferryman makes a connection between unremitting motion and spiritual death to question whether the American continent itself has not become a Ghoster, now in purgatory because of such misadventures as Braddock's defeat and the ongoing cutting of the Mason-Dixon Line, as consequences of the latter would soon include the Northwest Ordinance of 1785, an order that "provided for the surveying of the vast territory lying west of Pennsylvania and north of the Ohio River to the Great Lakes" (Danson 204). Pynchon's emergent nation in purgatory resists its own taxonomic drives and becomes a zombiescape that breeds dragons, serpents, and ghost-fish from its telluric constitution.

Captain Zhang senses that he has been hired by the surveyors to give them "yet one more hope in the realm of the Subjunctive" (*MD* 543). Pynchon associates this illusory realm with the Euro-American compulsion to superimpose pure mathematics upon a perplexing American wild in lands that have been rendered even more incalculable by decades-old boundary disputes, failed surveys, and royal pronouncements.[5] But the dragon or land's "true inner shape" (601) seethes with reactionary impulse to embody both the contingencies and prospects of Pynchonian space. Subsequently, to quote Arthur Saltzman, frontiers for the surveyors become increasingly "outlaw, dissolute, unfixed" to reflect a "fluxional reality that refutes their protracted ceremony of ordinance" (69). Pynchon's liminal America in *Mason & Dixon* holds out possibility for "open and unlimited" lands on the horizon despite the "disenchantment of America, the turning of the New World into just another part of the Old," which changes "subjunctive into indicative" (Cohen 275). But I disagree with the contention that subjunctive or Pynchonian space is the anticipated result of the American experiment in *Mason & Dixon*. Liminality takes us further. In the words of Dennis M. Lensing, *Mason & Dixon* "simultaneously enacts postmodern techniques, warns against the failings of postmodernism, and gestures toward possibilities beyond the limits of postmodernism" (142). To foster a new dimensionality of place, Pynchon, like DeLillo, uses postmodern conventions to postulate what Joseph Dewey characterizes as a "re-enchantment of the Earth as an animated creature and an overthrow of . . . the analytical system of oppositional logic that has centered Western thought since Descartes, indeed since Genesis" (123). In this light, *Mason & Dixon* depicts the earth as an unexpected source of transcendent signification, even as the surveyors find themselves unable to "inscribe a geometric sign of transcendence upon the Earth" (Millard 124).

Giants

As Pynchon's Golem and dragons show, the transcendence of place as totem and obscured presence in this novel manifests itself in gigantism. Giants in mythology and folklore largely have extraordinary physical power, they come from prehuman societies, and they are an inadvertent or direct threat to the humans they encounter. Residing just above humanity on the food chain, giants quite often serve their little friends as guardians or gatekeepers. No stranger to the lore of colossi, Captain Evan Shelby[6] tells the surveyors that the elaborate Serpent Mound he witnessed, presumably the mound near Brush Creek Valley, was "*already ancient*, by the time [Native Americans] arriv'd. Indians speak of a race of Giants, who built them" (*MD* 595). Native American scouts in *Mason & Dixon* regard the Giants as responsible for building the mound upon "the Fort at Redstone" (662), a landmark now referred to as Redstone Old Fort or Fort Burd, in Brownsville, Pennsylvania. Also "ancient when the Indians first arrived" (662), strongholds such as Redstone Old Fort were purportedly "built and later abandon'd by a nation of Giants, who possess'd a magick more powerful than that of the English or the French" (662). Strange hieroglyphic rocks, "Gigantick Bones," and recumbent monoliths around the fort give rise to stories of a race of giant people with "likenesses neither of Gods, nor of men,—but of Guardians [or] Helpers" (662) that according to legend will rise again "seeking to reclaim their Country" and "[r]edeem it" (662). When taken as a whole, these depictions of gigantism in Pynchon's novel offer a parable of environmental stewardship for the millennium: Americans must look to the past as a means to grow intellectually and morally to rise to the challenges of our ecocidal age. In so doing, there yet remains a chance to reclaim and redeem American lands in and around contemporary sites of destruction. The novel suggests readers must adopt the role of "Guardians" to avoid the Giants' fate of extinction, and as "Helpers" *communitas* with at-risk natural environments can be found.

Humongous vegetables and hemp plants also bloom on the Pynchonian horizon in a "place of Magick" where "Smoke comes out of the Mountains . . . the Earth rumbles [and] Springs of Fire run ev'rywhere" (654). Hugh Crawford[7] translates the words of a Mohawk tribesman who describes a distant valley where "Vegetables,—grow big,—very big. Big Corn. Each Kernel's more than a Man can lift. Big Turnip. Six-man crew to dig out but one. Big Squash. Big enough for many families to eat their way into, and then live inside all the Winter" (654). After learning about hemp plants large enough to serve as high-rises for spaced-out Indians, Mason and Dixon find "Indian Corn growing higher than a Weather-cock upon a Barn," flowers from squash plants that "they can jump into in the mornings and bathe in," and tomatoes that "tower high as Churches" (656). The Beet is not only colossal but has also attained something akin to enlightenment; the Head Gardener explains, "We are as Garden Pests to It. It suffers us. We being unworthy of Its full Attention" (656). The valley also emanates an odor "apotheckarial, œstral, musk heavy" where "one must bring along a Bladder fill'd with fresh Air, and now and then inhale from it, if one does not wish to swoon clean away, in these Gardens Titanick" (656). A secret sect of human gardeners attends to these plants for "Others who are absent, pending their Return" (656). Vegetal wonderlands left behind by intergalactic supergiants offer the surveyors deliverance from classification and scale, but not as mere utopian fantasy, Lovecraftian kitsch or antirational postmodernizing. Gardens "Titanick" become hyperbolic sites of engulfment where *Homo sapiens* can reconsider its niche within ever-changing global bodies. Being engulfed by gigantic flowers or vegetation in a way that is advantageous to the human—as opposed to conventional American pop-culture representations of invasion or contagion—offers for consideration an alternate and viable American history of mutualism and symbiosis.

Also Territory

Species itself enters the liminal phase in Pynchon's New World garden, as his "representation of crossed species boundaries—between animal and human, human and machine, vegetable and animal—challenges both scientific and popular categorizing by focusing on metamorphosis of species" (Hinds, "Animal" 181). And while it's true that *Mason & Dixon* "engages the taxonomic enterprise by representing species as hybrid and transforming" (180), the novel does much more than use hybridized monsters to point out shortcomings of the Enlightenment. Hybridization in this novel is not an entropic process that represents disorder and certain ecological dissolution; rather, "hybrid" species and landscapes function in a role akin to Bhabha's "*less than one and double*" (Bhabha 139), wherein the "boundaries of authority—its reality effects—are always besieged by 'the other scene' of fixations and phantoms" (166). This is the place where ecological identity is constructed in the face of signification to remind Pynchon's readers that place is always being born, not in a synthesis of binaries but in multidimensional interfusion. What might be called hybridity, then, tangles the conceptual lines between *Homo sapiens* and our fellow life-forms on paths to *communitas.*

In *Mason & Dixon,* "hybrid" creatures and spaces are much more than ontologically unstuck beings on a "sliding scale of species" (Hinds, "Animal" 183). When applying the factor of time or history to the concept of the ecological hybrid, we observe a "metamorphosis of species" (181) that leads to a betwixt-and-between state that Victor Turner describes as the liminal. Beyond a human-centered amalgamation of perspectives in one natural body to support a "newly pluralistic landscape of America" (Seed 92) and a refutation of the "right line," hybrid species in *Mason & Dixon* challenge readers to think of other life-forms and the landscapes we inhabit *as* embodied self. Here not only is the "earth . . . itself a creature" (Hinds, "Animal" 189), it is an organism both magnetic and miraculous made extant by not only animal, vegetable, and mineral adaptability but also mutable publics. To see ourselves as not only mind and body but also territory counters thinking that would taxonomize "hybridity out of official existence" and relegate "the hybrid to the popular sphere of 'monstrosity'" (Hinds, "Animal" 180). Ecocritically, hybrid "monsters" such as the Learned Dog, Felípe the electric eel, and "shape-'Morphers" (*MD* 491) such as werebeaver Zepho Beck signify a profound reunion with all life. Inside the bodily landscape, humans lose that part of the ego that says, "I am here, and you are there." This convergence makes it impossible not to embody the materiality of place, to share in its transformation.

The Wedge

Monstrous spaces such as the "Wedge" or "Delaware Triangle" also function as anomalous coordinates in *Mason & Dixon* to become "another of Pynchon's symbolic areas of anarchy, a place hospitable to the unofficial transactions that the culture attempts to suppress" (Seed 94). This "unmappable corner" (Cornis-Pope 142) near New Castle where Delaware, Maryland, and Pennsylvania converge remained in legal limbo for over a century as a result of misapprehension, avarice, and confusion from all levels of authority. This Wedge, or "Thorn," is described in *A History of Pennsylvania* (1973) as a stateless terrain: "[A] narrow wedge of land whose ownership remained undefined had been created between the western limit of the circle and the northeastern corner of Maryland—a narrow triangle of some 800 acres known as the Delaware Wedge or the Thorn. In 1921 Pennsylvania agreed to have this area and its inhabitants, who technically had never been the citizens of any state, formally transferred to Delaware" (Klein and Hoogenboom 188). This no-man's-land, argues Tony Tanner, is "clearly the kind of area favoured by Pynchon, and recreated in the generous, inclusive, permissive, endlessly surprising, secret-packed topography of his own prose" (*American* 223). But these readings of this "Geometrickally impossible territory" (*MD* 336)—in their desire to frame Pynchon's work as a historiography of democratic hope ironically laced with New Age idealism—overlook the environmentality of this and other odd places along the visto. For ecocriticism, the vexing parallax that exists inside the map's blank space reveals an increasing disconnect between topography and referent. As the purpose of a wedge is to separate two bonded entities from each other, a biocentric reading of this detached "Land-Scape" (542) offers the suggestion that Americans must first declaim the Wedge and then seek out its signified.

Subsequently, the movement westward makes Mason perceive the lands as increasingly eerie, as the crew fails to "mark the Boundaries between Reality and Representation" (429). Mason's ecophobia[8] makes him see the continent as "*invisibly connected*" (429) in psychogeographical formations that his astronomical tools cannot quite calculate. After Dixon dreams "of a City to the West" that is "busy, prospering, sacred," Mason replies:

> We trespass, each day ever more deeply, into a world of less restraint in ev'rything,—no law, no convergence upon any idea of how life is to be,—an Interior that grows meanwhile ever more forested, more savage and perilous, until,—perhaps at the very Longitude of your "City,"—we must reach at last an Anti-City,—some concentration of Fate,—some final condition of Abandonment,—wherein all are unredeemably alone and at Hazard as deep as their souls may bear,—lost Creatures that make the very Seneca seem Christian and merciful. (608-9)

At this point in the narrative, Mason articulates a fundamental paradox and logical failure at the heart of his project, one that finds a causal relationship between forested areas with low human population density and a moral disorder that requires clearing and constraint for the reinscription of natural law. From this paradox emerges a moral duty for Western mapmakers, missionaries, and colonizers alike to rescue the chaotic wild and its inhabitants by removing trees and other plant life. As the crew moves farther westward, "the darker side to the American landscape emerges," and Mason "comes to feel threatened by trees"; he "imagines the trees concealing malign and threatening presences" because, David Seed explains, "the trees literally cannot be surveyed" (89).

Colonel George Washington also sees a causal relationship between abundant plant life and moral terror when he mentally separates the "camp upon the Monongahela, and the Death-hollows all night from across the River" (*MD* 282). Washington describes the uncomfortable sensation of looking out at the "hollows" with a "long watchfulness, listening to the Brush [and] Ev'ry mis'rable last Leaf" (282). In the Pynchonian wilderness, there is more in the hollows than Native American "savages"; there also exists a phantom presence that both Washington and Mason associate with primordial malevolence. Washington assumes that Mason and Dixon will feel an uncanny eeriness when they "come to stand at the Boundary between the Settl'd and the Unpossess'd, just about to enter the Deep Woods" (282). This uncanny sensation results from viewing terrain, ecocritically, as Bhabha's "less than one and double," which is the experience wherein colonizer or mapmaker perceives the doubleness of place simultaneously as mirrored reflection of environmental hegemony and threatening utter wild. Like Bhabha's indigenes, ecosystems survive in *Mason & Dixon* through an elaborate process of mimicry and hybridization that both replicates and mocks the colonialist "fantasy of difference" (Bhabha 153); it is the detection of nature as mannequin or amalgam—the fetishized ecology thriving in the interstices—that makes Washington and Mason afraid of the woods. As Bhabha explains, hybridity "represents that ambivalent 'turn' of the discriminated subject into the terrifying, exorbitant object of paranoid classification—a disturbing questioning of the images and presences of authority" (162). Washington and Mason prefer nature as mannequin because they're spiritually separated from the bodily landscape, and they also equate comprehensibility with the virtues of use. But the "display of hybridity [liminality]—its peculiar 'replication'—terrorizes authority with the *ruse* of recognition, its mimicry, its mockery" (165).

Michael Harris agrees that "Pynchon anticipates the work of Homi K. Bhabha, who has moved the focus of postcolonial studies beyond rigid distinctions between colonizer and colonized into issues of ambivalence and cultural hybridity resulting from colonial rule" (206), and nowhere in this novel do we see such ambivalence and hybridity more pointedly drawn out than in the Mason-Dixon Line itself. Described in the book as "a living creature" (*MD* 678), the Line becomes a "tree-slaughtering Animal, with no purpose but to continue creating forever a perfect Corridor over the Land. Its teeth of Steel,—its Jaws, Axmen,—its Life's Blood, Disbursement" (678). This beast—"an hundred Blades all the day long" (678)—appears intent on "killing ev'rything due west of it" (678); seeing the stark destruction of the Line, indigenous people simply "want to know how to stop this great invisible Thing that comes crawling Straight on over their Lands, devouring all in its Path" (678). Dixon understands but Mason cannot yet admit that the Line has become a pretext for the subjugation of the New World through destruction and violence; Native Americans realize what "we" explorers "do to Trees, and how little we care,—imagine how little we care for Indians, and what we are prepar'd to do to you" (679). As Zhang has tried throughout this undertaking to convey, the Line is ultimately "a conduit for Evil" (701) that will be "of use at Trail's End only to those who would profit from the sale and division and resale of Lands" (701). "The forest is not an Agent of Darkness," Zhang attempts to explain to the surveyors, but "your Visto is" (615).

An ecocritical reading along this line suggests that though it would certainly be a stretch to describe Pynchon as a polemical writer of place, *Mason & Dixon* does call "for fellow humans to recognize the intractable, like-it-or-not interdependence that subsists between the human and nonhuman" (Buell, *Future* 102), to include our reliance on healthy environments for both physical and psychological nourishment. Pynchon scholars widely share the contention that the Line signifies resistance to the universalizing claim that "*terra incognita* must be rendered intelligible as well as geopolitically unambiguous" (Saar and Skirke 140–41). And though the Line "validates the surveyor's unconflicted vision for the landscape" as "the clearest sign of civilized human presence on the planet" (Saltzman 64), Pynchon exposes "in the line arrowing its way into the continent a host of portentous intimations regarding the future of the nation whose birth, as the surveyors take their sightings, looms on this historical horizon" (Cowart 342–43). Therefore, the Mason-Dixon Line truly becomes monster in light of contemporary environmental catastrophe. In the fin de siècle context of the book's publication, the Mason-Dixon Line "represents a misbegotten rational undertaking" that "promulgates the ideology of control" (Strandberg 107). Bearing witness to its consequences also inspires a meditation on the "erasing of lines, the blurring of distinctions, the proliferation of possibilities" (McLaughlin 191). Through the conjuration of omens proliferated by the Line, Pynchon offers the liminal to found a millennial ethos of stewardship in the aftermath of the atom bomb.

So as the meridian of Old World psychopathology cuts through consecutive bioregions by Mason and Dixon, the resulting visto becomes not a dead zone but—like the test sites and landfills in *Underworld*—a place of miracles. Pynchon writes in his 1984 review "Is It O.K. to Be a Luddite?" that to "insist on the miraculous is to deny to the machine at least some of its claims on us, to assert the limited wish that living things, earthly and otherwise, may on occasion become Bad and Big enough to take part in transcendent doings" (40–41). It is my claim that *Mason & Dixon* takes part in an important transcendent "doing" by traversing this shadowy moment in history to offer a "new, more hopeful story about America, emphasizing relation, connection, and possibility" (Cohen 265). As an ecocritic I agree with Samuel Cohen that *Mason & Dixon* does not require us to accept the inevitable dominion of the Line and that the novel "accepts neither paranoia or hopelessness nor unknowability" (283). These very tribulations, however, do plague Mason,[9] who at the novel's end speaks at once of the work of astronomer James Bradley and the New World itself: "'Tis a Construction,' Mason weakly [says], 'a great single Engine, the size of a Continent. I have all the proofs you may require. Not all the Connexions are made yet, that's why some of it is still invisible. Day by day the Pioneers and Surveyors go on, more points are being tied in, and soon becoming visible, as above, new Stars are recorded and named and plac'd in Alamanacks'" (*MD* 772). The bitter finality of Mason's remarks and the exactness of his dark prophecy offer little hope for the nascent United States, for failing to see this ever-shifting nation as a liminal creature is to blind oneself to its potential as place of renewal. But it is important to remember that Mason the father is not given the last word in this story, one told as a bedtime tale to children. It is his sons, William and Dr. Isaac, who end the book by telling their father that the "Stars are so close you won't need a Telescope" (773). The last two lines of the novel challenge readers to embrace the idealistic notion that America, this monster and place of dreams, is even now still being formed. Thomas H. Schaub speculates that readers "might ask of Mason's sons, What stream shall we go a-fishing in? The polluted stream of our present moment, or the time of the novel, which is to say in the remembered futurity; of a nation about to be born, the past already imperfect?" (201). But I believe Pynchon fishes where these streams run together, where the "remembered futurity" of a "nation about to be born" can return, like the transit of Venus, to reveal a world enlightened.

The Pocket

With striking parallels, Don DeLillo's panoramic and paranoiac post–Cold War novel *Underworld* provides readers with geographical and cognitive plots for reconstructing postnatural environments. Undermining linear history with a reversible chronology,[10] DeLillo's novel calls for a learned recognition of our malignant sites and wastes so that the United States might embrace its new domestic body in ways that preempt global meltdown. After a bout with cancer, we never know if malignancy will reemerge; after surgery there's no return to perfect symmetry. But to endure is to realize that the new body is always restoring itself,[11] and DeLillo's readers are challenged to acknowledge and even embrace this new earthly figure. In *Underworld* waste materials distort the map with protuberances and leaks that transmogrify the very meaning of landscape. But displacement behaviors and environmental delusions in the postwar United States are short-circuited in the novel by mammoth waste sites and mysterious toxic regions as well as land art that reanimates military machines. Existing as at least two places at once, DeLillo's liminal "white spaces" function between perceptibility and imperceptibility, seen and not seen. Shadowy regions like the White Sands Missile Range (WSMR) in southern New Mexico offer meditations on places where the "interplay of terrain and weapons" provides "a kind of neural process remapped in the world" (DeLillo 451). In 1974 the novel's Matt Shay works on the "lurid mathematics of a nuclear accident" (401) inside the "Pocket," an underground desert installation within the WSMR that tests weapons such as Pershing and Stinger missiles. Weaponized landscapes and subterranean bunkers provide DeLillo with a postwar theater of paranoia from which to explore how the cartographic imagination redesigns and completes the nation's more enigmatic sites. The missile range, a containment zone, houses laboratories where "bombhead" Eric Deming works in protective gloves and wears "layers of treated clothing equipped with a number of film badges and rad-detectors" (403). The laboratories are secured inside fortified buildings protected by concrete and lead walls, underground bunkers, guarded fence lines, security clearances, and vast deserts. Like rumors and conspiracy theories, radioactive contaminants are tightly controlled . . . but of course there are always slips, mishaps like the documented 1957 Albuquerque near-disaster that have the capacity to release both radioactivity and fantastic speculation.[12]

Near Alamogordo and Roswell, the "white places on your map include the air base, the army base, the missile range, the vast stretch to the northwest called the Jornada del Muerto and the interdunal flats as well—the flats were map-white, on the page and in living fact" (404). DeLillo's novel invites us not only to "read" desert landscapes that have been whited out by maps and fences but also to reinscribe upon the sand its viability as complex system. The bone-white sand dunes and dry flats of the Jornada del Muerto, like the Monongahela death hollows in *Mason & Dixon,* signify much more than a landscape of sterility and death. An uncanny wind transforms the desert in and outside the WSMR into a pregnant and monstrous expanse. It blows from the "Organ Mountains, busting up to fifty miles an hour, refiguring the dunes and turning the sky an odd dangerous gray that seemed a type of white gone mad" (402). When "the wind gusted out of the mountains," the novel importantly adds, "it rebodied the dunes" (416). Bombhead Eric details another sort of rebodying: the myelomas, adenocarcinomas, kidney failures, and hair loss suffered by "downwinders" who allegedly receive fallout due to occasional miscalculations. Wind releases particulate matter from inside the containment zone to "refigure" and "rebody" both human and environment as liminal monstrosities. The novel also reminds the reader that the "poets of the desert nations told stories about the wind. It bucks and swirls and turns you around and knocks you flat. But it also speaks so softly only your inner spirit can hear it and this is how you correct your path" (418). As phantom, the desert wind inscribes messages in sand dunes and human bodies alike to give the WSMR a chance to reconsider its own trajectory in light of history's arc. The windswept terrain also exposes American anxieties about poisonous dust and debris that threaten Cold War bodies trembling behind the skirts of global empire.

Bombhead

Unfortunately for the novel's myopic tech gurus, the wind's messages can be seen only by the "inner spirit" or, as Matt later finds, from outer space. Satellite photographs using color to identify terrain features reveal to Matt "signs of soil erosion, geological fracture . . . stress and drift and industrial ravage" (415); he also notes that "computer fuchsias or rorschach pulses of unnamed shades might indicate a change in water temperature or where the dwindling grizzlies go to forage and mate" (415). Landsat images show a planet under siege, but they also reveal a "secondary beauty in the world, ordinarily unseen, some hallucinatory fuse of exactitude and rapture" (415). Like the wind-fashioned bodies of sand dunes, the art of remote sensing replicates an atlas of environmental hazard and symbiotic promise, a mutable earth devastated by erosion, "industrial ravage," rising water temperatures, and habitat depletion. But it also provides an opportunity for us to *see*, as "hidden meanings" pulled from "out of the earth" (415) by digital maps make zombiescapes into transitional regions and prompt the fissure of outmoded ideological categories. Humanity, these images reveal, must draw from some future self unburdened by fantasies of Cold War dualism to conceive and refigure a world unseen.

Driving into the heart of a "wildlife preserve and gunnery range" (449)—another "white space on the map" (451)—Matt Shay and girlfriend Janet attempt to reconcile the desert's stark grandeur with its classification as militarized zone. In this "harsh and scarred" landscape, one can "almost read upheaval and convergence" (452); Matt frantically uses his field guide to identify birds, while Janet finds that she doesn't know "how to look at the desert" (449) because it is just "too big, too empty [and has] the audacity to be real" (449). Surrounded by "simulated tactical targets" (455), our postmodern campers are compelled at every turn to undertake a process of imaginative remapping to resolve the seeming paradox of cartographical white space as simulated post-tactical wildlife preserve.[13] They decide to sleep in a concrete bunker, their shared refuge from the incongruity of a liminal land that "was white sand and then red dirt, it was a cracked playa, drained and baked, and then it turned abruptly to mineral green dust and then again to sand and finally stony rubble" (455). The desert, with its hollowed mountains and underground missile silos, costumes its horrors as a "half-dreamed vision, the otherness of the West, the strange great thing that was all mixed in with nation and spaciousness, with bravery and history and who you are and what you believe and what movies you saw growing up" (449-50). But the hallucination born of the fabled American West no longer seems to work out there. After the Trinity test, its iconic mushroom cloud photographed on the parched horizon, the desert landscape's capacity to mystify the Western Hemisphere with cowboy pathos becomes increasingly ambivalent and fissile. In the face of "the thing with no name, the bomb that would redefine the limits of human perception and dread" (422), only some phantasm of the imagination might stay the fear that spreads "beyond the pushy extrusions of matter and into the elevated spaces where words play upon themselves" (251).

To See a Thing as Something Else

Matt's attempt in 1974 to reconcile the desert is taken up by his brother Nick in 1992, with better results. Seeking to reunite with landscape artist Klara Sax, waste manager Nick Shay finds himself at a desert art colony "at the edge of an enormous air base" (65), where Klara and her minions are painting hundreds of decommissioned military aircraft as a "landscape painting" that is the "landscape itself" (70). Known in art circles as the "Bag Lady" because of her use of "castoffs" and garbage as media, Klara is drawn to the desert because it is unconducive "to industry and progress" (71) and therefore can be declassified as waste. Klara senses that the US government shoots weapons at the desert because its presence is just too overwhelming to be processed by "technological culture" (70); like the bomb, the enigmatic desert is something that "eludes naming" and therefore must be relegated "to the status of shit" (77). The novel later explains that all "waste defers to shit. All waste aspires to the condition of shit" (302). If to map and name a thing is to own it, DeLillo suggests, the postwar United States has become coprophobic precisely because as a nation we've been unable to own up to our dark matter, the various noxious waste materials and broken lands dispersed and deserted since World War II. Advanced culture's sublimation of unspeakable shame requires that its littered and crater-marked desert ecology be seen as an isolated and meaningless collage, but Klara implores spectators to view her piece as "a single mass" (83). Recycling bombers as land art dares viewers to speak the unspeakable, face the shame of environmental and human atrocity, and reclaim the zombiescape as a vehicle for imaginative catharsis. Standing on a ledge to see the piece, Nick is astonished by the mass of abandoned military aircraft "arranged in eight staggered ranks" and painted in sweeps of "color, bands and spatters, airy washes, the force of saturated light" (83). Nick finds that the colors "did not simply draw down power from the sky or lift it from the landforms around us. They pushed and pulled" (83). This seminal moment when vision of terrain, sky, and art becomes unfixed is fundamental to this study because it enables Nick "to see a thing as something else" (64). What was once military waste has become a panorama recharged, and what once had the capacity to drop atomic bombs now fulfills a cultural desire to honor the forgotten by-products of an unsustainable culture and reanimate the debris for good. Recycling is an inspired process in *Underworld* because it reinscribes meaning onto the old World War II aircraft and thus can reclaim the desert itself. Klara describes "putting our puny hands to great weapons systems, to systems that came out of factories and assembly halls as near alike as possible, millions of components stamped out, repeated endlessly, and we're trying to unrepeat, to find an element of felt life" (77).

In *Underworld* the desire to "unrepeat" complex systems to refigure waste can also be seen in such historical sites as Watts Towers in Los Angeles and the Fresh Kills Landfill in New York. In 1978 Nick visits Watts Towers, the elaborate installation that creator Simon Rodia called *Nuestro Pueblo*.[14] Exploring this site, Nick finds himself haunted by the "towers and birdbaths and fountains and decorated posts and bright oddments and household colors, the green of 7-Up bottles and blue of Milk of Magnesia, all the vivid tile embedded in cement, the whole complex of structures and gates and panels" (276). Like Klara's land art, Rodia's hand-mortared "rambling art" with "no category" (276) is marked by the "cast-off nature of the materials" (277). In both works one finds that "a fertile anticipation emerges from a residual form" (Isaacson 55) in a way that prevents displacement and correlates the "felt life" of community with spaces and artifacts long discarded. Similarly, waste manager Brian Glassic feels "invigorated" (DeLillo 184) when standing on an "earthen bank" (183) watching Staten Island's Fresh Kills Landfill,[15] with its "garbage arriving twenty-four hours a day, hundreds of workers . . . bucket augers digging vents for methane gas, the gulls diving and crying" (184). As the wind pushes a foul stench across the waterway, Brian perceives that "the thing was organic, ever growing and shifting, its shape computer-plotted by the day and the hour" (184). And at this moment Brian feels "a sting of enlightenment" (184); much like Nick's ecosublime moment in the desert among abandoned aircraft, Brian has been spiritually captivated by the enormity and complexity of New York's garbage. If bioregional communities are to take responsibility for their own rubbish, these passages suggest, then let us artfully incorporate our garbage into the public milieu and "build hanging gardens here, make a park one day out of every kind of used and lost and eroded object of desire" (185). If "we point out where the waste goes," Timothy Morton explains, "we won't be able to keep ourselves from taking greater care of our world" (*Ecology* 51).

Leakage

But like Mason in Pynchon's novel, Nick only half realizes that he and his colleagues at the Future of Waste conference are willing accomplices in the push toward empire building and ecocide, enablers who hide underground toxins and radioactive secrets from the general population. While garbage does reveal to Nick and coworker Big Sims the fact that "everything's connected" (DeLillo 289), the monstrous desert landfill opens an ethical crater at the heart of DeLillo's novel that only Jesse Detwiler can truly fathom. Sims—a diligent corporate manager who confesses, "[E]verything I see is garbage" (283)—sees himself as "doing real work, important work" (283) but fails to grasp the larger implications of his "engineered crater" (285). When Nick stands looking over the gigantic hole, "five hundred feet deep" and "a mile across," he is "taken by surprise" and filled with a "weird elation" by the landfill's "drastic grandeur" (285). He is impressed by the massive layers of "artful plastic" that create a "prophylactic device" to prevent the surrounding soil from being steeped in contaminants (285). As an environmental literary critic, it's hard not to see the moment when Nick and the other men thrill at their mastery over this exposed orifice as symbolic gang-rape. DeLillo's description of the "polyethylene skin" that covers "most of the sloped bottom" (285) corresponds with the novel's musings on condoms, as the latex "technology they wanted to wrap around [Brian's] dick . . . was mass-produced latex they used to paint battleships" (110). Industrial-strength polymers and plastics are designed to provide protection for waste managers who want to put their junk in but don't actually want to come in contact, because to touch would mean accountability. As we learn from Nick's company, the appropriately named Whiz Co., it's much easier to bury your cast-off in plastic, discard it like a used condom, and seek out other sites. In a condom skit found later in the book but earlier in US history, Lenny Bruce jokes after rubbing and licking a "rubber" that this "is what the twentieth century feels like" (584), which suggests that the cutting-edge synthetic skin used by Americans to protect their genitals, battleships, and poisoned lands has given a false sense of separation and sterility that will ultimately lead to complications.

Jesse Detwiler asserts that over time Americans will feel a nostalgic need to return to their junk as a way to understand themselves, and he dreams about a postwar future that will make "an architecture of waste" (286). Detwiler the "garbage guerilla" (286) and "waste hustler" (287) believes that civilizations advanced throughout history because they had to cope with the problem of their own mounting waste. He implores his fellows to design "gorgeous buildings to recycle waste and invite people to collect their own garbage and bring it with them to the press rams and conveyors" (286). In this way, "waste is not rejected in a dualistic context, but accepted as part of a redemptive cycle" (Hardack 166) that transforms city planning and waste management into landscape art. Anticipating a green revolution in bioregional community building, Detwiler advocates unprotected intercourse with the liminal landscape to make our recognition of the environmental past part of a larger strategy of sustainable civil engineering. He explains that the time has come to "know your garbage" (DeLillo 286), which signifies not only acceptance of the toxic past but also a call to take responsibility for the abandoned objects and places that depletionist culture has long tried to forget. Elise A. Martucci contrasts Nick—who she argues overlooks the "problem of garbage when he gets caught up in the spectacle of the solution" (118)—and Brian, who at least gets that the "garbage . . . is real" (119). But I find it more useful to see Nick and Brian not as competing perspectives but as expressions of an intellectual process that both characters experience when confronting garbage as a liminal presence. In our desire to distance ourselves from our waste, both Nick and Brian suggest, we project our landfills and toxic sites to the margins of perceptibility, urgently seeking to affirm mental categories of environment, home, community, and body. But our refuse, still out there somewhere, once was (and still is) part of us. Christopher Todd Anderson explains:

> [T]he placement of our waste symbolizes the marginal status of garbage both as a material substance and as a concept. Because it includes both organic matter (such as discarded food, plant matter, and bodily waste) and inorganic material (including artificial products such as plastics and other manufactured items), garbage exists on the border between the natural and the artificial and, by extension, between human culture and wild nature. To the ecologist, borders between ecosystems—the seashore's intertidal zone or the margin where forest and meadow meet—are particularly worthy of study because of their abundant biodiversity. Garbage, too, is a liminal substance, existing as it does on the edges of human society. (35)

Like the test site, the landfill is a locus where culture's misspent past is interred so that it can be forgotten and contained. But despite our best efforts, the toxic region of the unconscious dreams of leakage and contamination. Like unused weaponry or a war zone, waste is the thing we thought we wanted but now wish to forget; humanity manages refuse by trying to make it into the place that is not seen and does not see. But rather than making a "remote landscape of nostalgia" (DeLillo 286) out of even the most dangerous garbage, waste managers in *Underworld* teach us that drawing the discarded world to the cultural center makes civilization less capable of living in denial and better able to recognize the "redemptive qualities of the things we use and discard" (809).

The Place in the Space

Part of the ecological liminar's metamorphosis in *Underworld,* a process that both Nick and Brian seek to comprehend, involves shaking off its status as "space." To become "place"—an important distinction for ecocritical readers—the limen must reject designation as blank repository for humanity's spiritual, psychological, and mercantile projections at a time in history when we are constantly led to believe that "capital triumphs over every blank space in the Other" (McGowan 135). Though critic Peter Boxall convincingly argues that "it is the sheer ingenuity of the novel's capacity to find value, sense and connectedness in the discarded, the random or the hidden that is one of its most miraculous achievements" (197), he uses confounding terminology when he argues that "the space of the boundary is both the space of death, and the space of possibility" (211). It is crucial for critics of modern and contemporary fiction to see the place in the space and find the garden apparent in the parking lot, the landfill, and even the abandoned missile range. David H. Evans explains that "the ultimate thrust of the novel is to direct our gaze away from the freakish and fantastic spectacle" of both postmodern and capitalist spaces in fiction and apprehend instead the real that "lies neglected beneath the mesmerizing parade of media-generated effects and virtual images that holds in thrall both consumers and cultural theorists" (132). Reality has moved to the cloud—leaders of nations no longer dream of "vast land empires" (DeLillo 787) but "want computer chips" (788)—and yet the earth persists. It is the truth of the underworld as it emerges from spectacle that enables the ecocidal imagination to bloom in our globalized and webbed-over minds, and this blooming is a first step to refashioning a sustainable world from materials once considered dead. Ruth Helyer explains that the "annihilation death offers collapses the borders between oneself and the world, flooding the body with the fluidity of its own insides" (990); abjection likewise "draws us to the place where definition disintegrates" (991). Indeed, the novel's "references to disposing of rubbish" as a way to "dispose of intrinsic parts of ourselves" (993) reveal ecological as well as psychological denial in the abject American zombiescape.

Rats

In *Underworld,* human suppression of its own outside is represented through depictions of landfill scavengers such as rats. In the criminal underworld, a rat is considered a vile character, liar, or snitch; the Norway rat, ubiquitous to areas of human habitation and waste disposal, likewise gets a bad rap. "When people tell rat stories," DeLillo's narrator explains, "the rat is always tremendous. It's a drag-belly rat the size of a cat" (194). Fabled rats can be "heard in the walls and down the yards, indelible half fictions, running across rooftops in the moon . . . in the sewers and demolition sites and coal bins, a rustling in the flung garbage of empty lots" (194). Rats provide an "endless source of stories, the size of the rats, the attitude of unfearing, how they ate the bodies of those who died in the tunnels" (440), and the landfill is described by Matt only half jokingly as "Planet of the Rats" (205). But despite the maligned sewer rat's less than savory reputation, let's remember that its relationship to humanity is inherently commensalistic. Its introduction to much of the world was a by-product of nautical trade routes—clearly not the rat's fault—and as a result the "natural habitat of the wild Norway rats is *wherever we are.* Human settlements are now the ecological niche of the wild rat: the farm, the city, the garbage dump, the sewer, the subway" ("Wild"). Nick tells the story of a date who exclaims after chasing a rat into a bathroom, "I am killing this fucking rat two times already! Rat poison with skulls! And now it is coming back!" (DeLillo 206). Like Pynchon's dragons and ghost-fish, the resilient rat is represented as myth, monster, and pestilence because it exemplifies the uncontainable within contested habitats, a nonhuman presence that creeps along walls, rooftops, sewer systems, and imaginations. Its depiction as multiplying, growing, gigantic, and slimy makes it an appropriate figure for American culture's consumerist and unsustainable history. But rats are fellow mammals that have responded to human development by creating an ecological niche alongside us. As liminal grotesques, DeLillo's rats are unaesthetic but vibrant and adaptive life-forms that flourish in postnatural habitats.

Museum of Misshapens

While doing business in the former Soviet Union, Nick begins to realize that all the "secrets kept in white-washed vaults, the half-forgotten plots—they're all out here now, seeping invisibly into the land and air, into the marrowed folds of the bone" (802–3). He characterizes a contaminated Kazakh Test Site as yet another "[w]hite space on map" (789) that "has to disappear somehow" (795). DeLillo's Semipalatinsk is a remote region where post–Cold War denizens "destroy contaminated nuclear waste by means of explosions" (791), which reminds Nick of the "curious connection between weapons and waste" (791). At the Semipalatinsk Polygon,[16] Nick wears his radiation badge and stares out at the aged towers, cratered "test dwellings," and "roads that end abruptly, weeds pushing through the asphalt" (793). He gorges himself on lamb and caviar at ground zero as the wind blows and the ground rumbles. Downwind, the Kazakhstan "Museum of Misshapens" (799) and the radiation clinic are entryways into a shamed place in DeLillo's underworld that commands witness: "There is the two-headed specimen. There is the single head that is twice the size of the body. There is the normal head that is located in the wrong place, perched on the right shoulder" (799). There are also survivors here: "the boy with skin where his eyes ought to be, a bolus of spongy flesh, oddly like a mushroom cap, springing from each brow" and the "man with the growth beneath his chin, a thing with a life of its own, embryonic and pulsing" (800). The bodies of deformed samples and orphans function as phantom presences that link organic structures with the tangibility of technological death. Brian chooses not to bear witness, but Nick bemoans the truth that it's the "kind of desperate crisis, the intractability of waste, that doesn't really seem to be taking place except in the conference reports and the newspapers. It is not otherwise touchable somehow, for all the menacing heft and breadth of the material, the actual pulsing thing" (805). But the ecocidal imagination, born in liminality, engenders "another kind of belief, a second force, insecure, untrusting, a faith that is spring-fed by the things we fear in the night" (817). Despite attempts to contain the dangerous contents of Cold War crimes such as nuclear tests at the Semipalatinsk Polygon, something always escapes through the cracks into local waterways and gene pools. The end result is a depiction of test site and landfill as repositories of enigmatic terror, places of disruption and mystification that can't quite be sorted.

Feeling "something drain out of [him]" (801), Nick is chilled by malformed Kazakh children's "faces against the landscape, the enormous openness, the breadth of sheepland and divided sky that contains everything outside us, unbearably" (802). He feels that these human and geographical bodies have the potential for both hysteria and transcendent function, because waste has become for him "a religious thing" (88).[17] Nick now sees "waste as something transcendent, a restored indication of the sacred" (McGowan 136),[18] and Detwiler predicts that the "way the Indians venerate this terrain now, we'll come to see it as sacred in the next century. Plutonium National Park. The last haunt of the white gods" (DeLillo 289). Mark Osteen postulates that toxic landfills "hide garbage under a cloud of unknowing that increases its dimensions and mystery" (227); the antecedent to the dual psychological mechanism's ecocidal imagination and transcendent function is paranoia, the process whereby all is ultimately accumulated and recycled. I agree with Paul Gleason that "DeLillo's nuclear waste land is a place of belief" (134) and that this novel "attempts to locate redemption in humanity's existential experience of a culture whose phenomenology is rooted in waste" (133).[19] But it's the redemptive quality of the liminal by-product—the waste itself—that has the capacity to elevate US culture to a cognizance of our current state. Nick reports at the end of the novel that the "landfill across the road is closed now, jammed to capacity, but gas keeps rising from the great earthen berm, methane, and it produces a wavering across the land and sky that deepens the aura of sacred work" (809-10). This "wavering" of methane gas and the way that it distorts the vision of the landscape embodies the conjunction of spiritual stupor, between-ness, and mania of literary figures—all waste managers now—who can't entomb the growing thing.

Some Nevada of the Mind

Paranoia, like the other manifestations of ecological identity projection in *Underworld,* is the mind's desire to see everything fit, connected. But Osteen explains that the novel "also dramatizes how waste cannot finally be contained" (216), because "physical and emotional waste are underground streams that always eventually surface" (227). If we are to approach place from the perspective of representative waste managers Nick and Brian, we acknowledge the position that if materials cannot be co-opted as consumer goods or sacred relics, their very existence has been a waste. And it is at this point that the limen—the test site, the landfill, or even garbage itself—becomes unclassified. While the novel makes obvious the truism that humanity can never really leave behind the more unsavory by-products of capital, the opposite is not true. If left alone for long enough, the white space on the map has the capacity to reincorporate itself into the surrounding bioregion and begin the process of healing. If the landfill were abandoned, birds and other scavengers would consume part of the waste, while the elements would begin wearing down materials to particulate matter. Flies and other insects would flourish, as molds, fungi, maggots, and plant life would get busy. This process would have little appeal from an aesthetic standpoint, to be sure, and toxins would linger for quite some time. But the point is that the landfill does not need us in the way that we humans require increasing amounts of clean water, resources, energy, and land. If left alone, the can on the side of the road will decay and become part of what we like to call landscape. Perhaps the fact that our refuse will survive us is one reason the clergy of garbage represented in *Underworld* appears so fixated on its potential for generating fear, reverence, and paranoia.

Nick's meditation on the word *waste* "suggests that both word and thing reach back to the roots of the culture, that they both have the capacity for metamorphosis, for reinvention; that they both return, insistently, in new forms" (196). The same can be said for post-ecological areas that have been at some point detached from bioregion, redefined as abject wasteland, and forgotten. The primary concern for ecocriticism is what becomes of unusable landfills and test sites after the most dangerous residuum has been sequestered in some Nevada of the mind. How do we as ecocritics—as people who rely on the planet's abiotic components to survive—foster the conception of these new spatial forms to promote such "reinvention" and "metamorphosis"? I believe that we must start with the understanding that the anticipated result of such an undertaking is *communitas*, or to use a term once popular in ecology, "climax community." When a natural area has functioned ecologically long enough for it to become "old growth," it has the potential to reach a steady state, the place that it was to become. One might even say that places yearn for climax, the actualization of their promise.

DeLillo's novel offers two possibilities for how humanity might move closer to such a climax community: recycling and decycling. Increasing numbers of Americans like Nick find comfort in separating glass from aluminum and placing the plastic bin by the side of the street. In Phoenix he marvels at the "impressive open-steel truss of the waste facility down off Lower Buckeye Road, with grackles sparking across the landfill" (DeLillo 803) and "showy desert plants spilling over the pastel walls above the parking area" (805) in "terraced gardens" (809). Waste sites such as the 27th Avenue Solid Waste Management Facility in Phoenix are part of larger sustainability efforts that engage the local community in conscientious garbage disposal. Nick likens the recycling center in the book's epilogue to a museum exhibit where, in the recycling shed, he and family members watch the "tin, the paper, the plastics, the styrofoam. It all flies down the conveyor belts, four hundred tons a day, assembly lines of garbage . . . square-edged units, products again, wire-bound and smartly stacked and ready to be marketed" (809). Liliana M. Naydan writes that the novel cycles in "expanses of waste, which move through cycles of rebirth through the recycling process" (179-80), and this "enables garbage to be born again—to reenter existence in a new life on earth and subsequently to face countless other ends" (190). In this way, recycling suggests a movement from liminality to climax. But despite the recycling center's great organizational achievement, it ultimately leaves Nick with an unpleasant feeling; he describes trucks "bringing in the unsorted slop, the gut squalor of our lives, and taking the baled and bound units out into the world again, the chunky product blocks, pristine, newsprint for newsprint, tin for tin, and we all feel better when we leave" (810). The wry use of "products again" and "marketed" makes it necessary for readers to "pause at this description of recycling's effects and question whether this 'redemptive quality' is a false sense of accomplishment linked to paradigmatic American attitudes toward production and consumption" (Martucci 121).

Perhaps a more useful description of refuse might be found when waste manager Jesse Detwiler offers his prophetic vision:

> I'll tell you what I see here, Sims. The scenery of the future. Eventually the only scenery left. The more toxic the waste, the greater the effort and expense a tourist will be willing to tolerate in order to visit the site. Only I don't think you ought to be isolating these sites. Isolate the most toxic waste, okay. This makes it grander, more ominous and magical. But basic household waste ought to be placed in the cities that produce it. Bring garbage into the open. Let people see it and respect it. (DeLillo 286)

The incorporation of these liminal bodies back into the structure of things not only transforms community through green civil engineering and architecture but also reforms our relationship to our discards by taking garbage out of hiding and bringing it back into public consciousness. To quote again from Catriona Sandilands's engaging article in *Ecocritical Theory: New European Approaches*, garbage can be reanimated by "violently wrenching salvaged objects out of their comfortable places in the mythic history of the commodity" and "gleaning them from their place in the trash can of bourgeois utility" (31). Through physical and neoaesthetic acts of reunification, *communitas* can occur because of the human reconciliation with estranged environments and the "salvaged objects" found within them. Here we must separate our garbage for recycling, sites for decycling. The joy of decycling is the pleasure of being unproductive, disconnected from capital—out to pasture, if you will. DeLillo reassures us in *Underworld* that "the world persists, the world heals in a way" (89), and the novel's final word embodies decycling as a form of climax and *communitas*. Martucci explains that the novel's "emphasis on place as identity shaper reveals the lasting significance of particular places in postindustrial society, no matter how altered or damaged these places may be" (141). But it is the identity of the place itself that concerns me, its status as limen being the agent that reshapes postnatural strata into something whole. Here, DeLillo leaves readers with a plausible arena to recognize and reclaim a state of harmony between humanity and landscape in the aftermath of the Cold War.

In his assessment of environmental literary criticism, Lawrence Buell asserts that it "will have been achievement enough if environmentality becomes seen as indispensable to how one reads literature" (*Future* 131). Underlying this statement is the hope that literature has the capacity to play a significant role in the restoration of consciousness and action needed to cope with our uncertain planetary berth. Environmentality in both *Mason & Dixon* and *Underworld* is bolstered by the recognition that the earth itself has entered a threshold not unlike Turner's conception of the liminal. What has been perceived as the end of the line is only the beginning. And the urgency and utter confusion of this symbolic transition leave literary studies with the opportunity to reconsider not only global processes of exchange and consumption but also the environmental impact of militant superpower.

3
Invisible Lands

Homecoming and Nativity in Ralph Ellison's *Invisible Man* and Derek Walcott's *Omeros*

Manuel Antonio National Park on Costa Rica's Pacific coast is a wonder. Packed with "postcard charms," it is described in the Lonely Planet guide to Costa Rica as a "place of swaying palms and playful monkeys, sparkling blue water and riotous tropical birds" (Cavalieri, Skolnick, and Yanagihara 317). Minutes after entering the Manuel Antonio Village gate to the park's "rainforest-backed tropical beaches and rocky headlands" (318), I saw a boa constrictor, colorful hummingbirds, iguanas, monkeys, zebra-colored grasshoppers, a hawk, and even a sloth. Brandishing a satchel full of illustrated field books, my knowledgeable tour guide expertly pointed out an amazing array of flora and fauna; he explained in detail the region's current ecological context and checkered history, to include the fact that these very lands were owned in the 1930s by the United Fruit Company. I was amazed to find that less than a hundred years ago this marvel of biodiversity had been razed as part of a banana plantation. Just outside the park, along the outer gate in Manuel Antonio Village, there's another liminal zone, a place of handwritten signs and ramshackle gift shops that I initially tried to ignore, because like most tourists I was excited to get through the park gate into the preserve to experience the *real* Costa Rica. At the gate Manuel Antonio Village becomes a bustling street scene of hucksterism and hardship, as elderly women wander through crowds of tourists selling colored bird whistles or coconut water, and "beer advertisements and barkers have inched right up to gates" (315). Sunburned men with stark faces sell the roadside for public parking as the "din from roaring buses, packs of tourists and locals hunting foreign dollars" reaches a "chaotic climax" (315). At this threshold, the bystander is both thrilled and ashamed. Martha Honey's *Ecotourism and Sustainable Development* (2008) reports that several parks on the Pacific coast, including Manuel Antonio, have "suffered environmental decay and loss of wildlife from far too many visitors" (172). She explains that Manuel Antonio, "whose curved, white-sand beaches and mountain backdrop have made it Costa Rica's most famous national park, received a staggering 216,000 visitors in 2005" (172). Despite its many resorts, restaurants, yoga salons, and souvenir shops, the "area around the park and the nearby town of Quepos both lack sewage systems, so refuse is dumped directly into the sea" (172). Some tourists at the gate turn their heads skyward and quick-march through the chaotic village to find refuge in the park, while other bewildered travelers are lured into the gee-gaw shops.

On trips to lush and exotic locales, it is imperative for privileged tourists never to actually be where they are—never see where they are—so that the fantasy of innocence may be preserved. The unspoken agreement between tourist and guide is that the fantasy gaze and postcard aura may not be complicated by social inequality or the environmental ugliness of such problems as the deforestation that typically occurs along the borders of popular nature parks where wealthy tourists are housed, fed, and entertained. To break the aura is taboo. Both books explored in this chapter make it their goal to break the aura, disturb the fantasy gaze, and press the viewer to recognize the truth of inequity and environmental injustice, to force the tourist-reader to recognize the inadvertent fraudulence of his/her gaze. When the fantasy is broken, these authors show us, spatial reanimation becomes possible. In *Invisible Man* native must become traveler, and in *Omeros* the traveler becomes native. In both cases the ambivalence of ecological liminality reveals a yearning for authentic reintegration into lands made invisible by environmental misuse. In both works the act of making habitats aesthetic or monstrous exposes social and ecological rifts that must be countered in symbolic homecoming.

Renowned for promoting environmental protection in his works, Derek Walcott encourages the West Indian island of St. Lucia to honor traditional practices and disavow industrial purse seining, land speculation, and the tourism industry. Depicting a community of "shipwrecked" islanders who often find themselves dispossessed in their own homes, Walcott's *Omeros* confronts St. Lucian sugar cane plantations and luxury hotels as parts of the same socioeconomic instrument. Underappreciated as an environmental writer, Ralph Ellison similarly details in *Invisible Man* how rural, campus, and urban sites are molded by conditions that cause human rootlessness, stagnate the rural homestead, and trap vulnerable bodies inside elaborate structures that sap agency. As yet unsung as an advocate for environmental justice, Ellison counters dispossession for African Americans on the farm, in educational systems, and those migrating to the city. From Europe's stretched shadow, both authors depict literary figures going on journeys beneath the earth's surface to reclaim both selfhood and home. Beauty becomes suspect in both *Invisible Man* and *Omeros* because images of picturesque people and landscapes too often obscure problems of racial inequality, poverty, and dispossession. To neutralize this effect, both books commingle abject bodies and ecological systems in rituals of mimicry and performance. The border dwellers and shape-shifters that emerge in both books are characterized as androgynous, undead, subversive, vegetative, and/or polymorphic. Homesickness in both *Invisible Man* and *Omeros* troubles liminal figures who must ultimately acknowledge their scars in rites of passage and begin the process of recovery. Ellison calls upon mockingbirds, starlings, and quail as well as vines to resist the nullifying effects of American social/civil engineering, and Walcott likewise summons fish ranging from king mackerel to blue albacore, as well as coral reefs. Both authors meditate on ants, depicting them in conflicting ways, as a means to better understand human function in shifting landscapes. And though Jack-the-Bear in *Invisible Man* is only beginning to wake up from his hibernation in the early 1950s, Achille and the other postcolonial inhabitants in *Omeros* anticipate a new morning where they might reconsider on their terms what home and habitat mean.

Jack-the-Bear

Kimberly K. Smith's *African American Environmental Thought* (2007) describes a black environmental tradition that emerges from folk narratives and takes shape through the work of luminaries such as Booker T. Washington, George Washington Carver, W. E. B. Du Bois, Jean Toomer, Charles Chesnutt, Richard Wright, and Langston Hughes. Just outside of the chronology of Smith's book, and as yet overlooked by environmental literary criticism, Ralph Ellison also deserves to be included as part of this tradition, because *Invisible Man* makes a considerable contribution to environmental thought in its own right. Ellison's masterpiece is keenly attentive to the way places of habitation have been molded and apportioned throughout the twentieth century, and his work is also highly sensitive to how dogma and ideology work within and through contemporary backdrops. One reason that Ellison has remained unobserved by ecocritics might be his complicated relationship with "agrarian types" such as Booker T. Washington and what he felt was a stultifying focus on rural life at his alma mater, Tuskegee Institute.[1] But regardless of his public disenchantment with the politics of soil, Ellison's *Invisible Man* offers keen insight into environmental blackness in the United States and speaks to the theoretical foundations of what is now known as the environmental justice movement. In *Invisible Man* resistance to environmental inequality is enacted by the narrator and other African American figures through performance and the conjoining of abject zones and bodies. Like García Márquez and Pynchon, Ellison conflates human physiologies with zombiescapes and phantom zones to propel his dark places into fruitful flux.

The Invisible Man's humiliating expulsion from college and subsequent journey to Harlem propel him into what critic Yonka Krasteva aptly deems a "liminal state, a process of transition and becoming" (71). As transitional body, the narrator takes an animal name; "Call me Jack-the-Bear," he remarks, "for I am in a state of hibernation" (*IM* 6). In terms of self-identification, Jack-the-Bear is a figure reminiscent of the stories of Joel Chandler Harris: "Jack," as in jackrabbit—the sly trickster—and of course the ever-plotting Brer Bear. Though now in a period of inactivity in his subterranean "hole," Jack-the-Bear will soon awaken, because, as he explains early in the book, "hibernation is a covert preparation for a more overt action" (13). Dormant Jack, who exists in an "ambiguous synthesis of stagnancy and change" (Krasteva 56), finds himself in geographical limbo because he lives, significantly, not "in Harlem but in a border area" (*IM* 5). As urban wildlife, his ecological identity becomes multiple and therefore blurry to the naked eye. On the most demonstrable level, the Invisible Man recounts the story of his betwixt-and-between state to authenticate his own humanity in the shadows of Jim Crow and scientific racism, to cure the "peculiar disposition of the eyes of those with whom I come in contact" (3). Rhetorical questions throughout the novel such as "What was I, a man or a natural resource?" (303) portray the puzzlement of rural Americans, black and white, who found it necessary during this period to reinvent themselves in the face of urban migrations, changing job markets, and rapid industrial advances. It's also true that the narrator uses his status as ecological limen to seek a nourishing relationship to the soil lost to him so that he might cure his sense of dispossession and help others. Shifting representations of both human and habitat in *Invisible Man* have the power to collapse the "center/margin polarity, turning the boundary, the in-between space, into a turbulent eddy, threatening to disrupt the traditional hierarchical arrangements" (Krasteva 56). And it is within this churning "eddy" that Ellison's stylistic countercurrent interrogates the college campus, highway, rural quarters, and city to find pathological landscapes and vertiginous zones in need of rescue.

Green Stretch of Campus

Largely derived from Tuskegee Institute, Ellison's historically black university is first and foremost styled a "beautiful college" (*IM* 34). In his underground lair, Jack-the-Bear recalls how the campus "grass turned green in the springtime and how the mocking birds fluttered their tails" as "white magnolias" enhanced the smells of "bee-humming air"

(34). But the most telling features of this aestheticized space—with its "roads gracefully winding, lined with hedges and wild roses that dazzled the eyes in the summer sun" (34)—are vines. The buildings are "covered with vines," while honeysuckle "and purple wisteria" hang "heavy from the trees" (34), and the "dry riverbed" is also "tangled with brush and clinging vines" (35). From this chapter's first passage an incongruity emerges, one that infects the psychogeographical heart of Ellison's novel and imparts its condemnation of beautified black landscapes. Just as the human body can become a site of performance and mimicry in exploitive cultural processes, lands possessed by African Americans in this novel must also perform. The beautiful campus becomes for the Invisible Man a domesticated and robotized zone, but one crawling with vines that in their liminality grow out of control. Much like the home gardens envisioned by Booker T. Washington in *The Story of My Life and Work* (1969), campus grounds during this period were meant to bring black students "into a proper relationship with nature, but the key point for Washington was that this relationship be the same as it was for white [students]" (Smith 92). If Washington's campus green serves as mime, as inferred from Smith, then Ellison's numerous vines are infiltrator "plants" that reveal the inability for the logic of landscape gardening to completely eradicate the region's potency and value. Instead, vines in *Invisible Man* embody the resistance of marginalized species to their herbicidal age.

As the narrator walks in memory through the ever-shifting campus, he encounters a number of suggestive animals. After noticing the "mocking birds," Jack-the-Bear recalls rabbits "so tame through having never been hunted, that played in the hedges and along the road" and "ants moving nervously in single file" (*IM* 35). Animals on campus have undergone behavioral changes in a zone of sterility that can impair, for example, rabbit defense mechanisms such as biting, clawing, and the evasion of natural predators. Rabbits of course are aesthetically appealing on campus and seemingly "happier" out on the green munching grass. But if a cat or coyote is introduced, domesticated bunnies are less apt to survive than those in the wilderness. Once shrewd and perceptive, Brer Rabbit has been tamed to the point of helplessness. Similarly, ants that typically emerge in spaces disturbed by human habitation walk in lines, communicating via pheromones toward sources of food waste and mirroring obscured college students who march "down the smooth asphalt" to the "chapel on Sundays," with "uniforms pressed, shoes shined, minds laced up, eyes blind like those of robots to visitors and officials on the low, whitewashed reviewing stand" (36). Biological and cultural bodies become automatized on Ellison's campus to produce both colonies and clones.

Another animal encountered in the opening pages of chapter 2 is the *Sturnus vulgaris*,[2] a bird known to make fascinating sounds and shapes in flocks during murmuration. Envisioning the "bronze statue of the college Founder," the Invisible Man remembers "his hands outstretched in the breathtaking gesture of lifting a veil that flutters in hard, metallic folds above the face of a kneeling slave" (36). This direct reference to *Lifting the Veil of Ignorance* (1922), the famous statue at the center of Tuskegee University of Booker T. Washington and a seated slave, makes the Invisible Man wonder in a much-cited passage "whether the veil is really being lifted, or lowered more firmly in place" (36). Somewhat different from the statue described by the narrator in *Invisible Man*, the partially enshrouded slave of *Lifting the Veil* is seated on a plow and anvil, holding a large tome, which signifies the relationship between working the land and social advancement at the core of Tuskegee Institute's historical mission. As the narrator gazes at the statue in memory, "there is a rustle of wings and I see a flock of starlings flighting before me and, when I look again, the bronze face, whose empty eyes look upon a world I have never seen, runs with liquid chalk—creating another ambiguity to puzzle my groping mind: Why is a bird-soiled statue more commanding than one that is clean?" (36). To see this passage as an act of desecration or "white face-ing" would be to miss not only its utter homesickness but also its wide-reaching environmental message. The world unseen by both Invisible Man and veiled slave is home, ironically made real in Washington's vision by the lesson to "dignify and glorify labor and put brains and skill into the common occupations of life" (Keck) written on the face of "the great leader and benefactor" (Keck) in "chalk" by birds. The "soil" left by the birds on the statue signifies not rural shame but the instructive quality of ecological design written like graffiti on domesticated spaces throughout the college campus. And it is the resulting ambivalence and confusion of the dispossessed experienced here by the Invisible Man that propel him into his journey as ecological limen.

The mimicry performed by the narrator in chapter 2 is reflected in the civil engineering of the "long green stretch of campus" (*IM* 36) where the grounds have been stretched and misshapen, molded like synthetic material to please the springtime millionaires who tour the college. The campus greens are also a stretch as ecological referent, which signifies for the narrator multiple levels of deceit beneath the façade. "If real," the Invisible Man asks, "why is it that I can recall in all that island of greenness no fountain but one that was broken, corroded and dry? And why does no rain fall through my recollections, sound through my memories, soak through the hard dry crust of the still so recent past? Why do I recall, instead of the odor of seed bursting in springtime, only the yellow contents of the cistern spread over the lawn's dead grass?" (36). This land of "thistle growing between the broken glass and sunheated stones" (35) alludes to the "heap of broken images" (Eliot 39) and "dried tubers" (38) found in Eliot's "The Waste Land," where the "sun beats, / And the dead tree gives no shelter, the cricket no relief, / And the dry stone no sound of water" (39). Healing water holds the redemptive and generative qualities needed to revive a corrupted and "corroded" campus; as Marc Singer notes, the Invisible Man "calls his university a 'flower-studded wasteland' and finishes his paean to it with a cry of 'And oh, oh, oh, those multimillionaires'" to parody "Eliot's line 'O O O O that Shakespeherian Rag'" (415). Through the eyes of tourist Norton, the campus itself becomes a "symbol of degraded modernity akin to the Rag" (415), but the Invisible Man admits the "grass did grow and the green leaves appeared on the trees and filled the avenues with shadow and shade" (*IM* 36–37). From this double vision, the campus becomes a land of the living dead, hidden behind a panorama of stretched lividity.

So it's apparent that the novel's conflicted representations of nonurban landscapes are partly an attempt to parse the environmental vision of such public figures as Tuskegee Institute's founder Booker T. Washington, who writes in *Working with the Hands* (1969) that the African American "pathway must be up through the soil, up through swamps, up through forests, up through the streams and rocks" (29). Washington himself maintains that he received his "first chance to get in touch with the real things in life" (9) when taking a job cutting a white woman's lawn "with a little hand-scythe" and removing every "weed, tuft of dead grass, bit of paper or scrap of dirt of any kind" (8). He recalls his pride "looking upon a yard where the grass was green, and almost perfect in its smoothness, where the flower beds were trimly kept, the edges of the walks clean cut, and where there was nothing to mar the well-ordered appearance" (9). Washington felt that personal dignity, cultural acceptance, and financial advance for his students were to be achieved in part by bringing physical space into proper proportion; both Washington and Ellison well knew that there was a performative component in the cultivation of so-called black landscapes. Washington thought the creation of tidy, self-sustaining homes where white people could see blacks living like idealized whites would improve race relations. This sort of thinking surely galled Ellison, who perceived the Founder's vision tantamount to pruning black identity in the agrarian Deep South at a historical moment when it was just starting to flower. From this backdrop the Invisible Man begins his journey from the campus to seek new and nourishing relationships to his home/land. Discovering this bond in his subterranean home, he recognizes that to "lose a sense of where you are implies the danger of losing a sense of who you are" (*IM* 577). In liminality, the Invisible Man struggles with the loss of ecological identity and thus intertwines social and environmental justice to establish a more genuine sense of self.

More a Shadow

Driving white benefactor Mr. Norton on a tour of the campus grounds, the Invisible Man enters an ecological twilight zone that will inaugurate his own journey as limen. To begin his rite of passage from docile student to ecological liminar, the narrator must first expose the black ancestral home as a performative site by returning with white witness to "cabins surrounded by empty fields beyond clay roads, and beyond a certain road a river, sluggish and covered with algae more yellow than green in its stagnant stillness" (35). The stagnant algae-filled water in this passage reflects not only the sluggishness of social and legal reform for African Americans in the heart of Dixie, but also the muddied relationship between himself and the rural. The Invisible Man's vision of the landscape, made double by the supposed all-seeing eye of Anglo authority, serves as an intellectual basis for Ellison's contribution to black environmental thought. As Smith details, the "black environmental tradition developed in response to two problems" (7):

> First, black theorists reasoned that race slavery and post-Emancipation racial oppression put black Americans into a conflicted relationship to the land—by coercing their labor, restricting their ability to own land, and impairing their ability to interpret the landscape. Second, the ideology of scientific racism that developed to legitimate this oppression promoted an environmental determinism that insisted blacks, as a race, had virtually no capacity for free creative action. (7–8)

The Invisible Man's aggrieved interpretations of landscape, as reframed by Norton's scientific racism, illustrate larger problems of dispossession, poverty, and unjust land distribution that prove key benchmarks for what would become the environmental justice movement. Ellison's novel of identity confusion and outsiderhood, in its defense of liminal people, provides an argument for rethinking invisible lands misappropriated and rendered infertile by the ideological machinations of plantation slavery, segregation, and environmental determinism.

On the rural road, Norton recalls that before the advent of the "great Founder" (*IM* 39), the "beautiful campus was barren ground" (38) and a "barren land" (39). Norton perceives the gendered earth around the campus lacking in value because of what he considers an insufficient level of production, and he also "apparently envisions himself as a fertilizer and redeemer of the once-barren land" (Singer 393). As Norton pontificates during his tour, the invisible narrator suddenly decides to "turn off the highway, down a road that seemed unfamiliar" (*IM* 40), a semiconscious act of rebellion intended to neuter Norton and offer this white man a new visual frame for the countryside. This particular back road, the reader finds, is in fact very familiar—even famous—to not only students and black sharecroppers but also whites in the area, because it leads to the house of the notorious Jim Trueblood. Off the highway, a "lone figure bending over a hoe on the hillside raised up wearily and waved, more a shadow against the skyline than a man" (40); the hoe bends this weary "shadow" to make this farmer an unhomely, ominous apparition in the garden rows. The Invisible Man also sees a "team of oxen hitched to a broken-down wagon, the ragged driver dozing on the seat beneath the shade of a clump of trees" (40); when asked if he can see the ox team, Norton answers, "I can't see it for the trees," but significantly utters that it's "good timber" (41). Ellison correlates the invisible forest—complex bioregion misapprehended—with phantom men and women in the Deep South who seek to work the land under inhospitable political conditions and very often without sufficient means to avoid the abuses of sharecropping and tenant farming. Reading chapter 2 of *Invisible Man* as a meditation on environmental justice prompts readers to experience the "recurring spectacle of poverty and suffering in the midst of natural beauty as undermining the value of that natural beauty" (Smith 55). Smith explains that "injustice does not only physically degrade the land but can also degrade the *meaning* of the landscape, and therefore the observer's moral relationship to it" (55). It is this attempt to assign value and meaning to unseen places degraded by misuse that leads the Invisible Man down this portentous back road and into the phantom zone.

When Norton fails to see the "ragged driver" of the ox team, the Invisible Man recalls, a "flock of birds dipped down, circled, swung up and out as though linked by invisible strings" (*IM* 41). At the road's edge, flocks of quail fly "over a field, brown, brown, sailing down, blending" (44). The use of the words "linked," "invisible," and "blending" to describe the unappreciated wildlife reaffirms the benefactor's blindness to an Alabama countryside that is prolific with both avian species and local wisdom. Only in recollection does the Invisible Man begin to understand the import of the quail landing at rest, safe at home in its camouflage of grass. Never incidental, Ellison's birds become precursors for acts of subversion. His essay "On Bird, Bird-Watching and Jazz" asks readers to "at least consult Roger Tory Peterson's *Field Guide to the Birds*" (Ellison, *Collected* 257) to better understand the relationship between jazz music and symbolic animals. "Mimic thrushes," Ellison explains, "which include the catbird and brown thrasher, along with the mockingbird, are not only great virtuosi, they are the tricksters and con men of the bird world. Like Parker, who is described as a confidence man and a practical joker by several of the commentators, they take off on the songs of other birds, inflating, inverting and turning them wrong side out, and are capable of driving a prowling ('square') cat wild" (258). Like campus "mocking birds" and statue-chalking starlings, flocks of birds along the highway embody a rural sensibility and symbiosis that Norton fails to recognize from the vantage point of his hired car. Beyond this avian threshold, sightless "square" Norton finds himself in a "new territory" (*IM* 46) where he is suddenly vulnerable to the "inflating, inverting" narrative of black bird Jim Trueblood, who, like Ellison's characterization of Charlie Parker, is both trickster and (con) artist. The birds appear to be in on the joke, though, as their songs and aerial improvisations offer both resistance and artful transport from Norton's "white line" (46).

Trueblood

Jim Trueblood in chapter 2 prefigures Rinehart as African American border dweller and liminal presence. Like Ellison's "Yardbird," Trueblood charms white audiences with songs filled with "earthy harmonies" and "crude, high, plaintively animal sounds" (47). A farmer who "told the old stories with a sense of humor and magic that made them come alive" (46), Trueblood is described as a man who "moved easily over the hot earth" and "covered the yard with a familiarity that would have allowed him to walk in the blackest darkness with the same certainty" (50). With a tourist's passing interest in Trueblood's slave-era log cabin, Norton inquires about the local inhabitants to find that "they say" (49) Trueblood impregnated his own daughter. Appalled and aroused, Norton has Trueblood recount a monstrous tale of incest and is utterly captivated by the "theater of Trueblood's performance" (Baker 177), which includes surreal dream sequences, gore, regurgitation, blood, and father-daughter sex. In its graphic exploitation of black bodies, Trueblood's "theater" echoes the novel's Battle Royal sequence in which African American men are made to enact violence upon one another for the fetishistic bloodlust of white authority figures. But unlike the victims of the Battle Royal, it is Trueblood who "inflates" and "inverts" abject depictions of rural black landscapes to his own advantage as both "trickster and merchant" (175).

Not surprisingly, birds and their calls offer insight into the ecocritical significance of Trueblood's tale.[3] Noticing that he's speaking as "though he had told the story many, many times" (*IM* 53–54), the Invisible Man observes, "Trueblood seemed to smile at me behind his eyes" (61) as if he's telling a different tale to each man. Trueblood recounts that as he huddles in the cold bed with wife and daughter, he hears a "whippoorwill callin'" and says to go "on away from here, we'll whip ole Will when we find him" (55). The whip-poor-will, a nocturnal bird rarely seen, due to its "cryptic coloring" ("Whip-poor-will"), becomes a bad omen. Trueblood reveals that his daughter Matty Lou "was grown," or sexually active; he wonders "how many times it'd done happened," just knowing "it was that doggone boy" (*IM* 56-67). Dreaming, he associates music "comin' from way, way off" with the boss quail "whistlin' tryin' to get the covey together again" (55). Despite the advancing hunter, the boss quail "got to round them up, so he keeps on comin'. Them boss quails is like a good man, what he got to do he *do*" (55). What Trueblood has to do—to keep his own "covey" together, shelter his daughter from "that doggone boy," and confirm his liminal status to whites—is to signify and scapegoat *himself* as racial archetype and totemic beast. In his bizarre dream Trueblood throws a woman onto a bed—a white woman trying to keep him out of a grandfather clock, no less—and "all of a sudden a flock of little white geese flies out of the bed like they say you see when you go to dig for buried money" (58). Trueblood enters the clock, stealing into history, if you will, to escape the white house but instead finds himself trapped in the bowels of some elaborate machine. Trueblood awakens at home to find that he is raping his daughter, which means, metaphorically, that his release can be made possible only through taboo and abjection. It is a moment of enlightenment and fraud, one that the Invisible Man comes to understand only at the end of the book when he grasps the meaning of "Rinehart."

As a plantation storyteller who tells hyperbolic tales on rural grounds where slaves once toiled, Trueblood is reminiscent of such literary tricksters as Chandler's Uncle Remus and Charles Chesnutt's Uncle Julius McAdoo. Trueblood's manipulation of the conventions of such tales suggests that the entire story of incest is a fabrication designed to not only con Norton out of money but also teach a complex moral lesson about the maltreatment of African Americans and their "haunts." If so, it's not altogether true that Trueblood "is the violator of boundaries who—unlike the scapegoat—eludes banishment" (Baker 183); as abject sideshow, Trueblood is deemed an outcast by both white and black inhabitants but allowed to remain in the region as a border grotesque. As an ecocritic I must quibble with Houston Baker's point that in Trueblood's "radically antinomian activities—incest, murder, and the destruction of sacred property—he symbolically captures what Turner describes as the 'amoral and nonlogical' rhythms and outcomes of human biology and of meteorological climate, that is, the uncontrollable rhythms of nature" (184). As liminal figure, Trueblood does not embody natural environment as disorderly taboo but rather as an organism susceptible to abuse. Ellison certainly represents the outside in ways that offer more than what Melvin Dixon deems an "artistic struggle to create meaning of chaos, which may be simply another word for wilderness" (56). More than simply chaotic, Ellison's wilderness is multifarious, sticky, and intimately woven into the Invisible Man's homecoming journey. From these passages it's abundantly clear that Tuskegee Institute and the surrounding area refined rather than dulled Ellison's understanding of the natural world and its role in progressive social movements.

In *Invisible Man* the outside does not create chaos, but what Valorie D. Thomas deems "vertigo," a sensation analogous to "'the unhomely moment' described by Bhabha in *The Location of Culture*" (82) that relates "the traumatic ambivalences of a personal, psychic history to the wider disjunctions of political existence" (11). Trueblood reconciles his own feelings of vertigo through abject performance, and his act perpetuates his liminal status because—as Jack-the-Bear later realizes—becoming abject "animal" can liberate one from both the name and identity imposed by rural campus or city. As limen the Invisible Man must recognize his own status as unhomely body and cure his vertigo by stabilizing the "unseen, liminal spaces of [his] experience by achieving internal equilibrium in a communal process of psychogeographical remapping" (Thomas 82). In this process, Shelly Jarenski shows, Ellison's narrator embraces "the social possibilities offered by abjection" (89) because the "process of bodily materialization produces, and even requires the production of, a realm of nonnormative, nonidentifying, and thus nonidentifiable bodies—a realm of the abject" (88).[4] But as abject presence the Invisible Man will offer much more than "an outside against which dominant bodies (bodies that are male, straight, and white) can be defined" (86); Ellison also includes landscape and nonhuman life as key facets of African American identity construction. And though it's true that the Invisible Man, like Trueblood, "consciously removes himself from normalizing forces and fully assumes the role of the abject," he plunges much further than "out of constructions of race and gender" (101). As unhomely body the Invisible Man also disrupts social constructions of species as he refigures landscapes constrained by plantation economics and corporate surveillance.

Soul Food

As he travels to Harlem, the Invisible Man enters a period of rootlessness that calls into question the relationship between dispossession and sustenance, to include a meditation on American cuisine. Food, especially soul food, is intimately connected in this novel to black identity as well as to feelings of shame. "I longed for home" (*IM* 260), the invisible traveler recalls as he walks streets filled with "confectioneries, luncheonettes, fish houses, and hog maw joints" (262); he sees "an odd-looking wagon, from which a stove pipe reeled off a thin spiral of smoke that drifted the odor of baking yams slowly to me," which brings a "stab of swift nostalgia" (262). Tasting a sweet yam dripping with "bubbles of brown syrup" (263) makes him "overcome with . . . a surge of homesickness" (264), but at least he is now able to eat the yam in public without being humiliated. The Invisible Man then fantasizes about "walking up and shaking a set of chitterlings or a well-boiled hog maw" (264–65) in the face of the college president who expelled him:

> "Bledsoe, you're a shameless chitterling eater! I accuse you of relishing hog bowels! Ha! And not only do you eat them, you sneak and eat them in *private* when you think you're unobserved! You're a sneaking chitterling lover! I accuse you of indulging in a filthy habit, Bledsoe! Lug them out of there, Bledsoe! Lug them out so we can see! I accuse you before the eyes of the world!" And he lugs them out, yards of them, with mustard greens, and racks of pigs' ears, and pork chops and black-eyed peas with dull accusing eyes. (265)

If Bledsoe were caught in the act of eating local food, insists the Invisible Man, newspapers would read "*Prominent Educator Reverts to Field-Niggerism*" (265), and he would "disintegrate, disinflate!" (265). Peeling back the yam—a tuberous root loaded with not only gustatory but also critical piquancy—reveals a deeper cultural tragedy, one that associates sustainable agriculture with not only *arrière-garde* social vision but also the obscenity and filth of the abject.

The Invisible Man's claim that "I yam what I am" (266) echoes Trueblood's "I ain't nobody but myself" (66), indicating for both figures a desire to subsist at the border regions so that invisibility might be used to realize an identity that resists, among other things, the admonishment of "field-niggerism." Growing and preparing bioregional foods are rituals of self-possession, an ethos Washington championed at Tuskegee and one that Ellison himself embraces in letters to Albert Murray. In Rome, for example, Ellison expresses his desire to find "some chitterlings" (Ellison and Murray 100), and he also writes a lighthearted story about "trying to cook a mess of pigs feet" (123) in Italy without proper pickling spice.[5] He is later delighted in New York to be entertained by Duke Ellington's sister, who had "a good down-home meal on the table—Yams, man! . . . Greens too, and all the fixings" (151). It's clear from Ellison's correspondence with Murray that both men have taken an aspect of rural life that might be seen as an embarrassment—a tradition of having to "make do" by foraging and eating seasonal vegetables without choice cuts of meat—and turned it into an interpersonal bond that draws from the past to inform their shared ethnic psychogeography. The novel's Invisible Man, however, cannot yet share in this bond; as he eats the yam, an "unpleasant taste bloom[s]" (*IM* 267) in his mouth, and he flings it into the street. The yam provokes his internal conflict with "that old agrarian self" (291) that has become a source of self-loathing, and the quandary of associating local food with the social injustice that facilitated its production continues what Dixon deems an "evasion of identity and kinship with the land" (71). This evasion is brought full circle, of course, when the Invisible Man takes a job and is "reborn" by machine in the Liberty Paints factory hospital.

Agrarian Zombies

After the Invisible Man catches the attention of the Brotherhood by giving a street speech on dispossession, sketchy activist Brother Jack refers to a family of former slaves as "living, but dead. Dead-in-living . . . a unity of opposites" (*IM* 290). Brother Jack likens the homeless blacks to "dead limbs that must be pruned away so that the tree may bear young fruit or the storms of history will blow them down anyway" (291). For Brother Jack, the agrarian zombie or uprooted self must be exterminated to allow for the march of social progress. Despite himself, the Invisible Man identifies with the beleaguered couple, their belongings piled like garbage onto the street. He notices "a pair of crudely polished bones, 'knocking bones,' used to accompany music at country dances, used in black-face minstrels; the flat ribs of a cow, a steer or sheep" and "pots of green plants . . . lined in the dirty snow, certain to die of the cold; ivy, canna, a tomato plant" (271). Interweaving motifs explored in chapter 2, "knocking bones" and vine-producing plants, suggest the performances and folk music of Jim Trueblood as well as the resistance of vines to the pillars of authority. Looking at the scant belongings, the Invisible Man feels "it was though I myself was being dispossessed of some painful yet precious thing which I could not bear to lose" (273). Paradoxically, it is the very "agrarian self"—this "painful yet precious thing"—coming out of hibernation from his repressed consciousness that compels the Invisible Man to become a community organizer and promote environmental justice in Harlem. Urban environments become central to Ellison's sardonic critique in the second half of the book and key to the Invisible Man's threshold experience as liminal body. Descriptions of Mary's apartment, for example, detail conditions of black tenants in Harlem, to include such concerns as sanitation, public health, pollution, and institutional racism.[6] At Mary's the Invisible Man awakens to a heatless room and hears tenants beating on the broken steam pipe, then sees a "small drove of roaches trooping frantically down the steam line from the floor above" (326). Later walking around the city, he is accosted twice for throwing away garbage and passes a toxic site that smells "of carbolic acid" (336); he also notices a line of trees and realizes that "cleared of its ramshackle fences and planted with flowers and grass, it might form a pleasant park" (377–78). But just as he envisions a garden in this polluted backlot, the Invisible Man notes, a "paper bag sailed from a window to my left and burst like a silent grenade, scattering garbage into the trees and pancaking to the earth with a soggy, exhausted plop! I started with disgust, then thought, The sun will shine in those backyards some day. A community clean-up campaign might be worthwhile" (378).

But in the wake of Ted Clifton's killing, the Invisible Man finds himself not doing community cleanups but torching a "huge tenement building" (545) with a group of saboteurs, many of whom live there. "You call *this* living?" (545) one arsonist asks of the decrepit building, and another says that his own child "died from the t-bees in that deathtrap" (547). Tactics employed by groups such as the Earth Liberation Front are used in *Invisible Man* to combat, among other things, tuberculosis, a disease that still infects people in poverty-stricken urban neighborhoods vulnerable to risk factors such as smoke inhalation, overcrowding, and malnutrition. As an eco-saboteur involved in a rent strike that later turns into a riot, the Invisible Man takes part in organized direct action against one towering symbol of environmental racism. But torching the contaminated slum apartment and merging with the carnivalesque street scene of looting and debauchery not only offer the narrator a chance to commit semiotic sabotage but also push him to the furthest depths of his struggle with his status as limen. He recalls after the tenement fire and his escape into a large crowd, "I was one with the mass, moving down the littered street over the puddles of oil and milk, my personality blasted" (550). But this violent blast that "provides the unease also provides the palliative" (Twitchell 34); like the symbolic transition from wound to cure in *Omeros*, the affected liminal exile "suffers from a lack of identity, a breakdown of self-consciousness, while at the same time there is the concomitant congealing power of the group" (34). However misguided, the violent act of subversion committed by the Invisible Man and his cohorts destroys the iconography of institutional racism—the slum apartment building or overpriced inner-city store—in an attempt to open the way for a more socially and environmentally aware city. Rather than trying to enter history as a means to "move out of the degradation of being defined as inhuman, or of no account" (Neighbors 235), the Invisible Man shakes it up with both the Brotherhood and the rioters to expose their monstrous conditions.

Rind and Heart

Ellison's Jack-the-Bear will leave his hibernation and return to the bonds of habitat and home, but only after he has morphed into a "mosaic self" who "learns to exploit the potentials of the void" (Krasteva

58). He will emerge at a time and place where "personal desires and social inscriptions intersect" (60–61), which is precisely the convergence that Turner describes as the transition from liminality to *communitas*. As both "mosaic self" and monster, the Invisible Man has learned to see the world through Rinehart's "green lenses" (*IM* 504) to finally recognize that his life is "one of infinite possibilities" (576). Ellison quotes Corinthians to describe seeing the world as both "rine and heart" (508): "For now we see through a glass, darkly; but then face to face: now I know in part; but then shall I know even as also I am known" (1 Corinthians, KJV 13:12). By giving both self and world a double take—by formulating an ecological identity that can draw from the interstitial regions of both consciousness and habitat—the Invisible Man will use routines, ruses, and multiple personae to assume a "socially responsible role" (*IM* 581) within his urban community. For Ellison, this role involves monkey-wrenching the ideological mechanism—the allegorical "robot" or "iron man" (570)[7]—that has historically stymied African Americans in their struggle to reclaim stewardship of homes and neighborhoods, to include green spaces. The Invisible Man "must shake off the old skin and come up for breath" (580), and when at the end of his tale he repeats the words "I am an *invisible* man" (*IM* 573), he recognizes that his tortuous journey from double-dealing southern landscape to littered Harlem ghetto has enabled his escape and given him the traits needed to return from underground. In the novel's epilogue the Invisible Man/Jack-the-Bear also acknowledges: "I've sometimes been overcome with a passion to return into that 'heart of darkness' across the Mason-Dixon line, but then I remind myself that true darkness lies within my own mind, and the idea loses itself in the gloom. Still the passion persists. Sometimes I feel the need to reaffirm all of it, the whole unhappy territory and all the things loved and unlovable in it, for all of it is part of me" (579). Interweaving his "mosaic self" with the "unhappy territory" south of the Mason-Dixon Line, the Invisible Man assumes a new ecological persona that can acknowledge and use the scars of history. He now sees the "American landscape not as pristine and innocent wilderness but as a corrupted land in need of redemption" (Smith 8). By having Jack-the-Bear emerge in the face of corruption, Ellison writes with veil lifted to redeem and honor the home that awaits. In so doing, he affirms this novel's valuable role in the African American environmental tradition.

Postcolonial Eden

Derek Walcott's *Omeros* also makes a vital contribution to ecocritical thought by depicting liminal figures who seek redemption through homecoming. Championing a return to the rhythms and reversals of

St. Lucia, Walcott's monumental literary achievement valorizes islanders who deny the lure of the disposable state—the "discos, the transports, the greed, the noise" (*O* 301)—and resist characterization of the Caribbean as mere tourist destination, untapped resource, or port of call. In Books Six and Seven, the island of St. Lucia is reclaimed by its larger biotic community through a process of spatial *nostos* that—as multivalent resistance to practices ranging from purse seining to the construction of luxury hotels—creates a renewed opportunity for the island and its inhabitants to heal. In so doing, Walcott moves ecocritical praxis "beyond nature writing, investing it with an ethical, future-oriented imagination that is necessary to envision and create future alternatives to ecological disaster and environmental catastrophe" (Braziel 124). St. Lucia's "future alternatives" hinge on a return of epic proportions; as Peter Burian argues, "*Omeros*, like the *Odyssey*, raises the question of what home means, but it does so in the context of the destruction of cultures and the erasure of identity" (369). Like Ellison, Walcott has cultivated a conception of home that must account for ecosystem destruction and the erasure of not only identities but landscapes. As liminal bodies, human and nonhuman figures in Walcott's poem must converge in interconnected journeys to find postcolonial Eden[8] in the gap between slave colony and tourist trap.

Walcott scholars have explored liminality as trope in *Omeros* to delve into issues of race and colonial rule.[9] The natural environment is often venerated in these works, albeit briefly, but most critics inadvertently support the anthropocentric approach of Anna Boyagoda, who feels that "region" in the poem is "presented as a natural container for community, but not as its cohesive force" (79). From a biocentric perspective, the "cohesive force" that Walcott's St. Lucian community founds itself upon can come only from "region," which can't be separated from the island's intricate aquatic and terrestrial ecosystems. I can't accept Charlotte S. McClure's contention that the "'O' as elegiac sound and shape" invokes "characters that continually reflect the island's changing from a pristine condition to one marred by tourists and commercialism" (17); I rather agree with J. M. Dash's argument that in Walcott's "reversible" St. Lucia the "poetics of liminality have taken the place of the pieties of maroonism" (148) and that the "liminal community" found in *Omeros* "now constitutes a new internal frontier, a site of transgression and growth" (148). These statements also leave the (biotic) floor open for a critical discussion of the "transgression" and "growth" of emergent biosocial frontiers. Perhaps the best place to start an ecocritical discussion of *Omeros* is with Ian G. Strachan's assertion that the "old imperialist vision of Eden, of so-called noble savagery and primitive innocence may be 'wrecked,' but an Edenic Experience of a new kind can be real," where "Caribbeans now find themselves in a New World, surrounded by an awe-inspiring nature, and they must start again" (193). But this new kind of "Edenic Experience" will occur only when islanders accept and merge with St. Lucia's "wrecked" and wounded body in the liminal stage.

A Parodic Architecture

In *Omeros,* clues for finding this new paradise can be found in nonhuman life-forms such as coral. Healthy coral reefs are central to the vitality of St. Lucia because they protect its shorelines from tropical storms and hurricanes; the fishing industry also depends heavily on biologically diverse reef ecosystems. Walcott's thalassic world surrounding St. Lucia supports "self-healing coral" (*O* 296), which forms "a parodic architecture" that has "re-erected the earth's crusted columns" (296). Walcott implores readers to look down below the water's surface to find a structural grandeur even older and more dynamic than architectural wonders such as the Parthenon, grand edifices erected to signify the preeminence of Greek civilization. Designs created by St. Lucia's vivid and biodiverse coral reefs are "parodic" because they exaggerate ancient temples and ornate theaters that, in their excesses, attempt to defy imminent decline. Unlike the cold and static beauty of marble, liminal coral "feeds on its death" (297) to grow and expose cracks in cultural and civil engineering formations that have lost sight of bioregional materiality and wealth. The coral reef in *Omeros* offers an important way to understand Walcott's vision of a new St. Lucia, as the liminal island and its inhabitants are challenged to reclaim "earth's crusted columns" as "coral parthenons" (297) by using natural decay as nutrient source and structural material. After coral dies, Walcott writes,

> . . . the bones branch into more coral,
>
> and contradiction begins. It lies in the schism
> of the starfish reversing heaven; the mirror of History
> has melted and, beneath it, a patient, hybrid organism
>
> grows in his cruciform shadow. (297)

In this passage the "contradiction" of new life brings with it possibilities for a polymorphic island that can soften and even reshape the "mirror of History." The baggage that comes with St. Lucia's shameful past as slave colony can be dispensed with outright if people heed examples found in sites of renewal such as reef ecosystems. Walcott suggests here that in the subaquatic "shadow" of exploitation, a "patient, hybrid organism" grows that will redeem his island home.

Achille's Garden

Walcott couples St. Lucia's life aquatic with Achille, the fisherman who goes on two separate nautical journeys that serve as psychogeographical rites of passage. During his first crossing—a sunstroke-inspired return to Africa—Achille becomes a water-breathing "walking fish" (142) and travels three hundred years "under the translucent belly of the snaking current" through "vast meadows of coral, / over barnacled cannons whose hulks sprouted anemones" (142). As shape-shifter, Achille descends to the nautical underworld and lives beneath the translucent equatorial currents that separate Africa and the Caribbean. On the sea floor Achille finds that one historic symbol of Old World dominion in the Caribbean, the cannon, has been overtaken by a rich proliferation of sea life. The "snaking" ocean offers Achille historical knowledge of the limits of imperialism through the sea's powers of reversibility. Achille's shadow is "reversed" on the sea floor to rest "over his eyes / like a grazing shark" (142); in ascension, he can "see his own shadow in the coral" as "his fins spread their toes" (142). Back at the surface, Achille transforms from fish back to mammal when his shadow returns to the coral. If Achille "is an Odysseus and the voyage is his *nostos,* his return home" (Burian 368), the sea is now "Achille's garden" (*O* 234), and St. Lucia his larger body as he and the island together awaken.

When Achille returns to consciousness in his canoe, he sees amongst Philoctete's catch that a "kingfish, steel-blue and silver, / lay fresh at his feet" (157). The kingfish, an overt reference to the Fisher King of Arthurian legend, offers the sacrament of traditional livelihood to bring vitality to the suffering island. Jahan Ramazani explains that like the "Fisher King in Eliot's *Waste Land,* Philoctete is a synecdochic figure for a general loss, injury, and impotence that must be healed for the (is)lands to be set in order. If Philoctete is the Caribbean Fisher King, Achille plays the role of questing knight who must . . . rejuvenate the wounded fisherman, the land, and its people" (*Hybrid* 58). But the quest to revitalize St. Lucian bodies, ecologies, and people becomes the charge of not only Achille but all members of the community, to include "self-healing" terrestrial and aquatic environments as well as human figures such as Ma Kilman, poet "Walcott," Omeros, Seven Seas, Major Plunkett, and Philoctete himself. Perhaps even more important to Walcott's narrative of reanimation is the fish "gaping" (*O* 157) in the bottom of the canoe. The poem describes the eye of this king mackerel as like "a globed window / ringing with cold, its rim the circular river / of the current," and its "cold eye in sunlight [. . .] blind as the moon" (157). The eye of a blue albacore is also noted; its "grey lens" clouds "the gaze of the albacore," its "blue flakes yielding the oceanic colour / of the steel-cold depth from which it had shot" (157). Eyes of sacrificial fish stare up at their human captors as witnesses, which as written suggests that if Philoctete fishes for personal consumption and local trade, the fish are exultant in death and the island is redeemed. When caught in the old way, the fishes "yield" the colors of the sea to Philoctete.

Walcott explains in "The Argument of the Outboard Motor" that rather than viewing nature within Wordsworthian or Miltonic frames, "we have to update nature. A canoe is a beautiful thing in St. Lucia, the object which is hollowed out and has great elegance and speed. So there is the emblem of a canoe going across the sea with a man on it, and it is a great image and something organic" (129). He suggests that when the outboard motor is added, the speed of catching fish may increase, but the "subtlety" of the organic relationship between human and ecosystem gets lost. Moreover, Walcott speculates that if "you let your outboard motor be your equivalent of, say, a hotel, of a skyscraper, of a big building, of another something that paves the ground and pays no attention to the contours of the earth, then you have the architectural question of what you are doing to the landscape" (130). Healing becomes wounding and wounding becomes healing by degrees, a paradox that Walcott seeks to reconcile in Books Six and Seven of *Omeros*. It's also important to note that neither fish species described in this passage is currently classified as endangered, though both are notably at risk of overfishing by the commercial fishing industry. For fishermen who still use "the old ways," their work is "prayer." They "caught only enough, since the sea had to live" (*O* 301), and their age-old fishing methods are described as both sustainable and divine.

"The king going home" (159), Achille says about a distant "frigatebird" as the fisherman returns from his first journey; both his psychical return from Africa and Philoctete's catch will contribute to the anticipated success of the multivalent vegetation ritual that St. Lucia must undergo in its liminal phase. It's important to note that Achille's second homecoming narrative in Book Seven occurs within the context of climate change, silver mining, purse seining, and aquatic species loss. Seven Seas bemoans "strange weather" (299) in which the "rain had lost its reason / and behaved with no sense at all" (299–300); moreover, Achille observes that the climate's "changing / was beyond his strength," and the "wisdom was enraging" (300). In these passages Walcott seeks to report on climate change not as abstract political narrative but as events observed by indigenous peoples who are intimate with island rainfall, temperature, humidity, and tides. Enraged with these erratic changes, Achille sails south "away from the trawlers / who were dredging the banks . . . for silver" (300), which is of course both the color of valuable fish trapped in the trawl net and the corporate wealth those fish will net. He also witnesses "banks robbed by thirty-mile seines, / their refrigerated scales packed tightly as coins, / and no more lobsters on the seabed" (300); the poem clearly relates purse seining and other industrial fishing systems that use "voracious, insatiable nets" (300) to seafood depletion in the Lesser Antilles. In search of "not Rome but home" (301)—not empire but habitat—Achille and Philoctete continue to head south toward the Grenadine Islands until, gloriously, their boat is lifted into the air by a massive baleen whale. Achille now "has seen the shut face of thunder," experienced death, and "seen the pod / burst into spray" (303). In this second journey, Achille's passage leads to a sublime recognition of his own extended biological family and his responsibilities to it; he and Philoctete turn "home, their wet, salted faces shining with God" (303). Isabella M. Zoppi explains that the "radiant appearance of a whale at the end of a day's fishing . . . lights up [Achille's] maturity and rediscovered wholeness" (519). Achille will now protect the island by consecrating traditions such as canoe fishing and the *paille-banane* dance. He will also claim Helen's child, whose paternity "is unimportant" because "coming to self-knowledge, the island Self recognizes that it is part of an archipelago" (Burnett 293).

Green Pretense

Ecocritically, Walcott's exculpation of long-established methods exposes what might at first appear a counterintuitive attitude toward local environmental practices. From its opening pages, *Omeros* does not shrink from disquieting representations of ecologically destructive acts such as cutting old-growth *Aniba firmula*, the island's "tall laurels" (*O* 4). Philoctete and the other men become "murderers" (3) when they "wound" (3) the *laurier-cannelle* trees, and as they cut and dismember the laurels with their axes there's "blood splashed on the cedars" (5). Such violent imagery in passages heavy with Homeric undertones would seem to indicate that in the act of tree cutting both St. Lucia the "island laureate" and the men lose honor and fame. Moreover, Walcott describes these trees as the indigenous Aruacs' "pillars that fell" (5) to make clear the connection between the island's threatened ecological future and its cultural past. As St. Lucia's "first god was a gommier" (5), a gum tree, it's difficult to see the passage as more than a denouncement of "the decimation" (6) caused by the "remorseless axe" (7) that hacks "limbs from the dead god" (6). But Walcott associates this wounding of the forest with sunrise, a "light of sacrifice" (5) that will leave "a blue space" (5) in the "hole the laurel had left" (6). Like kingfish sacrificed to nourish the island, downed trees that are crafted to become fishing boats ensure that these "trees are animated even in their death, animated by a desire to be of use, and through that desire, presumably, they become canoes" (Lock 14). The "blue space" or "hole" left by the crown of trees is Walcott's zone of liminality, the remains of a place "destroyed as a necessary sacrifice, out of which a new culture is born" (Hanford 765). Here the poem makes a much broader statement about the relationship between the environmentalism of wealthy nations such as the United States—where Brazilian rain forests become little more than media talking points—and indigenous people who use techniques such as slash-and-burn to grow crops in infertile soil. By describing small-scale fishing and forestry by St. Lucians as virtuous, and by putting these acts in the context of late-twentieth-century environmental collapse, *Omeros* draws attention to the pretense of environmentalists who live in industrialized contexts and certainly enjoy a standard of living that affords them electricity, cars, and nice homes—but who would inadvertently deny subsistence farmers in developing nations the opportunity to grow enough to eat. By singing the praises of Achille and Philoctete, Walcott underscores far worse ecological crimes associated with not only seine fishing and big timber but also the tourist industry.

The Cure

Perhaps an even more important Odyssean journey in *Omeros* is undertaken by Philoctete, the wounded fisherman who is healed by obeah woman Ma Kilman and does the traditional *paille-banane* dance. Philoctete's foul wound, made by a "rusted anchor" (*O* 4), is "puckered like the corolla of a sea-urchin" (4) and described in Book Six as the "flower on his shin" (235).[10] As the corolla of a flower consists of its petals, Philoctete's wound echoes both kingfish and *laurier-cannelle* in that his scar will invariably lead to the restorative ecosocial flowering of the island. Ramazani explains that by using "metaphor to leap the gap between destruction and healing, Walcott's language performatively converts injury into remedy" (*Hybrid* 67). Because Philoctete now signifies "his natural island environment in the Caribbean" (56), the healing of Philoctete's wound is Walcott's metaphorical catalyst for phantom St. Lucia to re-emerge in environmental *communitas*. As postcolonial Eden, Walcott's St. Lucia will draw from its diverse human populations, nonindigenous species such as the sea-swift, and lessons learned from its destructive history to craft a healing island that will adopt reclamation as stewardship model.

Recovery by acknowledging with scars from the island's slave past.[11] To cure Philoctete with her special potion, Ma Kilman in a sense *becomes* island in a liminal zone where "[t]opography and human geography converge" (Wyke 362). Ma Kilman must also journey to find a mysterious plant for a vegetation ritual enacted in Philoctete's medicinal bath. If Helen functions in the poem as an island mirage of imperialist fantasy,[12] Ma Kilman embodies the adaptability required for island life to flourish independently of such projections. Embracing an eclectic herbalist Christianity informed by African folk traditions, Ma Kilman draws on beliefs that "furnished the unifying forces—myth, ideology—that made the slaves' prolonged collective resistance to the plantation system possible" (Benítez-Rojo 160). Donning a "black hat with its berried fringe" (*O* 236), Ma Kilman searches through herbal remedies such as "Hail Mary marigolds" and "thorns of logwood" (236), but the "furious sibyl" (237) can't remember where the rarest and most potent healing nettles might be found. She must travel up the "rain-cracked path" (238) into the deepest wood to find a "plant that originates in Africa, and whose seeds had been carried to St. Lucia by a sea-swift" (Fumagalli and Patrick 67). Her trek up the mountainside leads to healing vegetation as well as African divinities—"Erzulie, / Shango, and Ogun" (*O* 242)—whose powers as Yoruba and voodoo warrior deities have faded with the passage of time. Robert D. Hamner theorizes that Ma Kilman's "quest" is also "enhanced by animistic overtones" when she observes a line of ants moving up the path "drawn to the same objective" that leads her "to the inland heights" (134). Contrasting the robotic hymenoptera in *Invisible Man,* Walcott's ants "serve as one more link in the organic chain because the African plant in St. Lucia sprung from a seed dropped by a migrant swift lures Ma Kilman and an army of ants back to the healing earth" (134).

But the organic convergence Walcott describes is possible only because of the unnamed plant's foul stench, as Ma Kilman finds the medicinal flower by following its noxious smell. The power of "gods in the leaves" (*O* 242) is concentrated "in the whorled corolla of that stinking flower" (242); the smell of the African plant, like the pain of having to trudge through nettles, signifies the discomfort and sacrifice that both postcolonial islander and wounded island will endure in their shared rite of passage. Ma Kilman's invocation from the "agonized O" (246) of the mouth of a sugar mill cauldron comes significantly in the "language of ants and her grandmother" (244). To find the natural mixture required to cure Philoctete, the obeah woman must mutate and become a monster herself; she rubs dirt into her mossy hair and bays to the stars until she turns into a "tree of snakes, the spidery sibyl / hanging in a sack from the cave at Cumae" (245). Ma Kilman the mutable prophetess bathes Philoctete "in the brew of the root" of the unnamed plant until he can "feel the putrescent shin / drain in the seethe like sucked marrow" (247). This is the poem's moment of St. Lucian origin, of genesis or dawn, when a new island is born.[13] Walcott explains the moment in this way: "The Adam idea is not an industrial theory. It won't work in that environment, but what it does do, I think, is it cherishes the environment, and if it's properly cherished, then it gives something to the cherisher. Obviously, to write with that in mind in the Caribbean . . . brings the concept of a beginning, of another day, the beginning of the possibility of another kind of culture, another kind of civilization" ("Argument" 131). When Philoctete rises from the sacramental cauldron, it is fitting that Walcott deems him "Adam" and writes that the "yard was Eden. And its light the first day's" (*O* 248). Like the other writers studied in this book, Walcott refuses a "static Eden, a fixed Paradise" and imagines instead a genesis that is "plural, becoming, autonomously flowing, and above all, dynamic" (Braziel 123). In Walcott's postcolonial paradise, wound becomes seed, and the phantasms of history are exorcised in liminality to celebrate the island's rebirth.

For the cure to spread, the bodies of Philoctete and Achille must become catalysts during Christmas festivities in an elaborate dance that provides an opportunity for the island to act out its status as ritual liminar in a carnivalesque street scene. To perform the *paille-banane* dance, both men adorn themselves with "calabash" and "rustling banana-trash" (*O* 273) to become vegetable hybrids.[14] Achille smells "like a flower" (274) and "unswaying cedars" (276) to dispel the island's foul stench and redeem its blooming, resilient biota. Described as "androgynous warriors" (276), the spinning dancers have taken female characteristics; Achille wears Helen's "tight lemon dress" stuffed with rags for "breasts" (275). The "island itself thus becomes an androgynous trope" (Burnett 295), which indicates that neither the narrative of male heroism nor stale "constructions of nature as female" that maintain "hierarchical ways of thinking" (Legler 228) can succeed here as metonymic reagent. Paula Burnett infers that the *paille-banane* dancers "are not the poem's only androgyne. The island-body itself, imaged initially as female, takes on maleness" (295). As he performs, Philoctete is "blent / to his rite" (*O* 277) in a "strange blurring of edges" (Callahan 64) that unfixes him in limbo to become a vessel for the transubstantiation of human and biotic communities. Fumagalli and Patrick explain that though "healing has an individual process" in modernity, the result of cure is homecoming, "to return to the community and to one's work, though as (re)new(ed) men" (68). Moreover, as Charles W. Pollard notes, "after his cure Philoctete is more often referred to as Philo, a renaming that evokes his renewed capacity for brotherly love. . . . He is healed enough to serve the community" (187). By becoming postgendered ecocentrics in carnival, the *paille-banane* dancers also reveal the importance of the nonhuman in island identity formation. The "subterranean and subversive space provided by the carnivalesque" in *Omeros* not only challenges the "dominance and ideology of colonial modernism" (Gikandi 187) but also provides ecocritical grounds where bioregional germination can begin.

Inland flora and fauna must also survive "wounds" leveled on Walcott's liminal St. Lucia. Book Six opens with descriptions of plants besieged, as "feathered lances of cane" are "spears" in "squared fields," like ranks of soldiers that echo "distant rain / marching down from the hills" (*O* 221). Militias of cane—the biological remnants of colonial sugar plantations—converge with "cannonballs of rotting breadfruit" (224) found on the nearby ground. Breadfruit, a nonindigenous plant species brought from the Pacific to feed slaves in the West Indies, enables the poet to see both:

> a past, they assured us, born in degradation,
> and a present that lifted us up with the wind's
>
> noise in the breadfruit leaves with such an elation
> that it contradicts what is past! (223-24)

Breadfruit leaves in the wind signify, in the "twin-headed January" of the New Year, a degradation that becomes "elation." In this passage one cannot ignore Walcott's integration of nonindigenous plant life with the legacy of human castaways in the Caribbean; animals such as ants and iguanas also communicate the island's state of flux, as both "speak" to the poet in languages inflected with both Darwinian wisdom and communal sensibilities. For Ma Kilman, as noted, it is the "line of ants at her feet" speaking in a "language she could not recognize" (238) that helps her find the healing plant left by the seaswift. "In the sounds of the natural environment," Joseph Farrell argues, *Omeros* "finds a linguistic source that is indeed older than language itself" (264-65). Omnipresent iguanas and other lizards also offer a "linguistic source" for the island's Aruac past. They bear witness to tree cutting in Book One and emerge "like tongues from the mouths of cannons" (*O* 312). Victoria Carchidi importantly states that the "lizard, symbolic of the island before colonization, lives beside the flower from Africa, brought by the swift that crisscrosses the globe. The natural world can bring these elements together, nourish them, and develop new life" (185). Inland plants and animals in *Omeros* communicate past injustice so that human islanders might rethink their collective lives as they experience liminality as rite.

Soufrière

The crisis of duality, limbo, and intermediacy that makes the vulnerable island also a site of promise manifests itself most explicitly in the figure of "Walcott," the poet who must visit the underworld to experience spatial *nostos* and then use his own craft to shape the postcolonial Eden he foresees. Like Homer's *Odyssey* and Ellison's *Invisible*

Man, the "Walcott" passages in *Omeros* detail the "story of a man having a hard time getting home" (Walcott, "Reflections" 230), and Walcott explains that this hard time is true for all Caribbeans who have found themselves "in a shipwrecked condition" ("Argument" 133). Like Crusoe, "shipwrecked" St. Lucians also have a chance to experience the Adamic act of renaming; Walcott writes in "What the Twilight Says: An Overture" that people of the Caribbean "must begin again from the bush. That return journey, with all its horror of rediscovery, means the annihilation of what is known" (25-26).[15] In *Omeros* this threshold experience is performed in Book Seven, "where Omeros/ Seven Seas leads the poet through a re-created Dante's *Inferno* that is layered onto the landscape of St. Lucia" (Prior 584). This trip to the underworld begins when "Walcott" sees a mutable figure on the shoreline that keeps "shifting shapes, or the shapes metamorphosed / in the worried water" (*O* 280), which suggests that the poet has come to a threshold that will expose the liminal nature of his own island identity. As tourist "Walcott" follows the gaze of his Homeric guide eastward to the sea, he finds:

> . . . I saw no shadow underline my being;
> I could see through my own palm with every crease
> and every line transparent since I was seeing
>
> the light of St. Lucia at last through her own eyes. (282)

The poet's lost shadow here signifies the surface beauty or untapped wealth that he and many other lost souls have used throughout history to frame and harness St. Lucia for personal gain. "Walcott" can "see through" his own deceit now as island becomes mirror; transforming into a biocentric seer, he can now "at last" see the island outside the prism of his own desires and ego. Like Philoctete, "Walcott" feels "every wound pass" (282) as he begins to evolve from tourist into native. Drifting with Omeros/Seven Seas and a ferryman reminiscent of Charon, the poet must journey past "the shore's / dividing line" (285) to Soufrière volcano and then bear witness to "hell in paradise" (289). Importantly, Omeros/Seven Seas sings that Soufrière is "a volcano, stinking with sulphur," which makes "it a healing place" (287). Like Philoctete's scar, Soufrière has a "brittle scab crusting its volcano's sores" (289), and the stench of the island's wound for a second time becomes a therapeutic bath. Soufrière is the island's wound and flower; it is the foul-smelling place that sparks healing and revival.

Festering inside this geothermal abscess are the damned souls of St. Lucians who receive poetic justice in foul pits much like the vile ditches that entomb the fraudulent sinners of Dante's Eighth Circle.

In the "Pool of Speculation" (289), those "souls who had sold out their race" (289) are traitors "who, in elected office, saw the land as views / for hotels" (289); another villain "had rented the sea / to offshore trawlers, whose nets, if hoisted, would show / for thrice the length of its coast" (290). Included in the volcanic mire are a hotel magnate who sees "his purple sea / as a postcard archipelago with gnarled pines / and godless temples" (290), and the detested colonial sulfur miners Bennett & Ward, whose ampersand between their names is "coiled like a constrictor round the tree of Eden" (292). It is essential to note that the gravest sins in Walcott's St. Lucian underworld are real estate speculation, industrial fishing, and tourist development. Hector is also found in Walcott's inferno, "shouldering the lance of an oar" (292) with a "shield like a spiked hubcap" (292); he too suffers the Soufrière Malebolge because in life he abandoned his canoe to become a driver for tourists. We gather here that tourism in *Omeros* projects both aura and fantasy onto the landscape because it abstracts and renames the destination locale, making it a doomed servant to what Burnett calls "tourism's production of neo-colonial cultural and commercial dependency" (291).

Without a doubt, this poem goes through hell to help the island avoid servitude and escapist fantasy. The poet notices "coastal villages receding" (*O* 227) and being replaced by a corporate paradise where even the "gold sea / [is] flat as a credit-card, extending its line / to a beach that now looked just like everywhere else" (229). Tourists crush the "immortelle's vermilion / platoons under their sandals climbing to the redoubt, / from where they shot the humped island with its blue horns" (311); the language of war seen in the opening stanzas of Book Six returns in Walcott's description of reckless vacationers. "Platoons" of flowers are crushed, and the island is "shot" to render it "paralyzed in a postcard, a concrete future" (227) as St. Lucia starts to become "a souvenir / of itself" (310). But though much of St. Lucia's "life adjusted to the lenses / of cameras" (311), it is Achille who refuses to "strike a pose / for crouching photographers" (298) and therefore does not lose "his only soul to the click of a Cyclops" (299). Heroically, Achille at this moment reproaches the misuse of exotic Caribbean islands by writers and readers as well as holiday travelers. Natalie Melas adds: "Most readers of *Omeros* are also potential tourists, wittingly or unwittingly consumers of Caribbean leisure space or of the inescapable and seductive representations of the area in advertisements, with their redeployment of the familiar colonial tropes—enchanted island, pre-lapsarian paradise, Robinsonnade and the romance of the shipwreck, the plantation fantasy of complete dominion, the racial fantasy of complete mastery" (155). The tourism industry projects an imaginary world "as paradise islands, images of desire, dream locations where innocence and beauty can be recovered" (Burnett 291), but to sell this "world," this aestheticized zone, the actual ecosystem has to be supplanted, remodeled, or rubbed out. The more tourists gravitate to the picture-perfect simulacrum of the Caribbean, we gather from *Omeros*, the less the phantom archipelago will resemble its waning referent.[16]

Another volcanic pit has been left for poets who see "only surfaces / in nature and men" (*O* 293); like real estate deals and the tourist trade, Walcott's poetry contrives bucolic images to render aesthetic fragile ecosocial constructs. "Hadn't I made their poverty my paradise?" (228), the poet asks regarding the islanders, and derides his own "hypocrisy / of loving them from hotels" (228). Like the tourist, Victor Figueroa explains, the "poet is . . . bound to the dispossessed by his or her very position of privilege" (33). In his Nobel Lecture, Walcott laments that the traveler "cannot love, since love is stasis and travel is motion. If he returns to what he loved in a landscape and stays there, he is no longer a traveler but in stasis and concentration, the lover of that particular part of earth, a native." In *Omeros*, Seven Seas says to "Walcott" that "you have seen / nothing no matter how far you may have travelled" (*O* 291), and the poet realizes that "the right journey / is motionless; as the sea moves round an island / that appears to be moving" (291). As poet, then, "Walcott" must also come home and cease his travels to reclaim and rewrite Eden as native. Paralleling Achille's return from the sea floor and Philoctete's emergence from the healing bath, "Walcott" awakens from his own underworld journey in hopeful elation. Significantly, Philoctete hails the returning poet with "Morning" (295), which shows that an important barrier between them has been broken. This hailing does not simply affirm the poet's subject position but reminds "Walcott" of his importance as island niche. In his Nobel Lecture, Walcott also describes a "force of exultation, a celebration of luck, when a writer finds himself a witness to the early morning of a culture that is defining itself, branch by branch, leaf by leaf, in that self-defining dawn, which is why, especially at the edge of the sea, it is good to make a ritual of the sunrise." When considering this St. Lucian dawn as both homecoming and opportunity for healing, Walcott's sunrise takes on ritualistic significance to draw together human figures—Achille, Philoctete, and Ma Kilman, as well as the Plunketts and Helen—with the self-healing island to create paradise in the light of communitas. "You know," we learn from Walcott, "the grass that emerges from the ruins is the grass that says it's beginning again" ("Argument" 133).

4
The Future Has Not Yet Begun

Apocalyptic Bodies in Robert Kirkman's *The Walking Dead* and Margaret Atwood's MaddAddam Trilogy

Since the release of George Romero's 1968 cult classic *Night of the Living Dead,* zombie narratives have obsessed over the building of barriers to keep out undead monsters and separate neighborhood, home, yard, and woods. They're also about the collapse of those barriers in graphic violence.[1] The post-Romero onslaught in American popular culture has unleashed hordes of hungry ghouls grasping through fences and broken windows in search of animal protein at a time when population and food security concerns loom on the global horizon. In the epicenter of this contemporary zombie swarm,[2] Robert Kirkman's comic series *The Walking Dead* probes claustrophobic spaces, flimsy structural barriers, and all sorts of ghastly permutations of the human body. In a world burdened by destructive storms, erratic demographics, extreme temperatures, and fears of a post-fossil-fuel planet, mass zombification is a telling expression of American anxieties over ecological security on a global scale. Margaret Atwood's MaddAddam trilogy also dwells on the consequences of current environmental practices on contemporary landscapes; like Kirkman's comic, Atwood's trilogy offers not only a prophetic warning but also a handbook for post-apocalyptic survival. Though Kirkman's ghouls and Atwood's genetically modified creatures reflect the zombified and bioengineered environments readers have come to associate with end times, both *The Walking Dead* and the MaddAddam trilogy take pains to explore undead cities, suburbs, small towns, and wilderness areas to point out interstices where optimism and even utopian dreams are possible.

American Zombiescape

Kirkman's graphic series moves cultural allegory beyond the sociopolitical struggles found in Romero's "Living Dead" films, such as civil rights in *Night of the Living Dead* (1968), commodity culture in *Dawn of the Dead* (1978), class inequality in *Land of the Dead* (2005), or excesses of post-9/11 militarism in *Survival of the Dead* (2009). In *Land of the Dead,* which I consider the most eco-conscious movie from this list, zombies led by ghoulish patriarch "Big Daddy" attack corporate tower Fiddler's Green; Kirkman's creatures, on the other hand, migrate and hunt in decentralized flocks or swarms. Romero's *Land* retains a corrupt militant social order that uses money within an urban gated community, but Compendium One of *The Walking Dead* focuses on rural and wooded areas within a forage-and-barter-based economy. "Stenches" in *Land* are beginning to engage in art and civic action, but Kirkman's "roamers" and "biters" exhibit a range of animal behavior patterns. Though *Land of the Dead* and *The Walking Dead* are arguably the two most important pieces of zombie lore in the post-9/11 West,[3] Romero's film is constrained by the logic and urban planning of the twentieth century. In contrast, *The Walking Dead* offers readers a millennial backdrop to introduce issues of animal rights, species extinction, food depletion, and climate change. By depicting zombies, survivors, and lands as liminal entities moving toward some larger collective outcome, Kirkman's comic revives natural environments by mentally eating away at the integument separating human and place. The resulting graphic violence and gore are traumatic reminders of the elemental, flesh-bound constitution of *Homo sapiens* so that readers might reflect upon our exceptionalist attitudes toward other species and our fragile lives as liminal beings.

From their death and resurrection, zombies have always been associated with American spatial conflict.[4] The Caribbean or Deep South plantation operated by zombie labor in films like *White Zombie* (1932) has been replaced in *Night of the Living Dead* by the farmhouse overrun by bio-zombies or ghouls, and the sinister, mysterious bokor or "boco" of Haitian lore now looks a lot like the industrial military state.[5] And while it's true that "the zombie remains purely a monster of the Americas, born of imperialism" (Bishop, *American* 38), the millennial zombie emerges from an age of global pandemics, WMDs, industrial pollution, fears of human overpopulation, and climate change. Therefore, ghouls in *Night of the Living Dead* and its progeny differ from the *zombi* of Caribbean and South American origin in that, to quote Kyle W. Bishop's *American Zombie Gothic* (2010): "(1) they have no connection to voodoo magic, (2) they far outnumber the human protagonists, (3) they eat human flesh, and (4) their condition is contagious" (94). Unlike Haitian zombies, post-Romero ghouls often swarm in self-organized herds or packs to repossess social and ecological spaces. Infection is a precondition of existence in *The Walking Dead,* and thus the "dead corpse of anyone that dies for any reason will reanimate as a zombie, unless the brain of that individual is badly damaged or destroyed. When a person dies, the virus they carry reactivates critical areas of the brain that support necessary vital systems, resulting in reanimation" ("Zombies").

We gather from these characteristics that the contemporary zombie narrative reflects American fears of viral contagions, global food supplies, mysterious meat production, and the effects of industrial pollutants. Brought upon by McModernity, *The Walking Dead* uses famished corpses to lobby for healthy, safe nourishment for the world's people. Zombie bodies serve as stand-ins for lands depleted by progress, as Nick Muntean explains: "Much as some of these collective anxieties expressed through the zombie center around the disturbing dialectical reality of modern social progress—that society's technological development is only attained by a concomitant increase in the potential for society's own self-destruction—so, too, is the zombie creature a liminal figure, simultaneously both life and death, and yet not really either, a monstrous 'degree zero' of humanity that defies easy categorization or explanation" (82). Muntean's description of the zombie is important for ecocriticism because terrain also reaches "degree zero," which means that the entire backdrop of *The Walking Dead* defies classification to disturb the "dialectical reality of modern social progress." Like the human undead, settings in the series resemble working ecosystems but show telltale signs of decomposition and toxicity; as liminal bodies the landscapes are "neither living nor dead from one aspect, and both living and dead from another" (Turner, *Forest* 97). Like human ghouls, many of the zombiescape's functions have atrophied—diverse species and natural resources eliminated—and only the lowest level of functionality remains. Apocalyptic nature becomes undead when in an ontological blur it begins to mimic and distort healthy ecosystems.

This blurring of spatial ontology clouds the ethical and legal distinctions separating human and nonhuman life, which can give some critics the creeps. Paraphrasing Karl Marx in "The Idle Proletariat: *Dawn of the Dead*, Consumer Ideology, and the Loss of Productive Labor," Bishop argues that the "feckless individuals living in Romero's mall ultimately lose that which makes them essentially 'human,' and they regress to a more primitive, animal state" (235). He feels that Romero's zombies "do not organize or act according to any kind of plan; any autonomy they manifest is a direct result of the instinctual drive to consume" (237), because "lower beings have nothing beyond the activities that preserve and sustain life" (244). I believe that Kirkman's zombies pose a challenge to this easy (and false) dichotomy separating humans and so-called lower beings by both putting humanity in elemental crises and infusing zombies with characteristics of other lifeforms. Compendium One depicts monstrous humans, humanoid creatures, and phantom lands as liminal entities in a process of perpetual destruction and renewal. "A figure for environmental crisis," Greg Pollock explains, "cannot be like a human Other, someone or thing different we stand against. Rather, this figure would constitute itself as a

Figure 1. Swarming, *The Walking Dead*

series of reversibilities within the subject, so that what appears at one moment as victim appears at another as monster" (175). Zones of spatial reversibility in *The Walking Dead* make the zombie a striking figure for environmental decay and revival; when the line between extant and extinct becomes confused, humanity must create an entirely new land ethic and in so doing redraw the parameters of human identity.

A Pandemonium of Post-Affluence

On a behavioral level, zombies in *The Walking Dead* have more in common with seagulls in Alfred Hitchcock's *The Birds* (1963) than with Romero's living dead. Ecocritically, *The Birds* draws on the American fear that other species of life might still have some dominion over landscapes that have been neutralized by modern progress. Hitchcock's film picks away at species hegemony by having seagulls, ravens, crows, and sparrows conspire to reclaim the coastline and town of Bodega Bay. Hitchcock's birds and Kirkman's zombies are effective killers in flocks when they swarm, encircle, and bite their human prey. Animated aerials, perched angles, looming birds on a shrinking periphery, and eyeless corpses in *The Walking Dead* all parrot Hitchcock's avian apocalypse, while raids on the farmhouse by multiple attackers—creatures that break through doorways and windows—could allude just as well to the work of Hitchcock as to Romero's. Like Bodega Bay's migrating fowl, zombies are beasts that, after being introduced to an area, experience a population spike and subsequently feed on human beings as proxy nutrition source. Like angry birds, walkers attack as a response to shifting geographical borders and changing food supply, indicating a shift in *The Walking Dead* from humanoid ghoul to zoological limen.

Liminality is also expressed through refugee migrations along a graphic topology where final destination or community is serially thwarted. In this journey the reader is required to imaginatively grapple with real-world difficulties that accompany environmental breakdowns such as food and water scarcity, lack of electricity, and inconveniences as mundane as dirty clothes. In a pandemonium of post-affluence, a new world is being fashioned to advance *The Walking Dead* beyond mere survivalist fantasy into considerations of local agriculture, post-American selfhood, and the structuring of a sustainable society. Julia Round asserts that the "story of *The Walking Dead* is about the ongoing survival of its protagonists, rather than the dreadfulness of zombification" (164), but Kirkman doesn't reduce "survival" to human protagonists in conflict with zombies and "the dangers of the natural world" (165). Rather, the natural world actually *becomes* protagonist and must withstand mass migrations of refugees, species collapse, and major shake-ups along the food chain. As a result of an ecocidal global culture, the zombie makes death a catalyst for cultural transformation in part because it challenges the notion that the zombie isn't truly alive because it lacks human consciousness. Turner notes in *The Forest of Symbols* that "much of the grotesqueness and monstrosity of liminal *sacra* may be seen to be aimed not so much at terrorizing" but in making participants "vividly and rapidly aware of what may be called the 'factors' of their culture" (105). As an unlikely agent of *communitas*, the zombie pulls human culture into a state of vivid terror "accompanied by experiences of unprecedented potency" (Turner, *Ritual* 128). By depicting the liminal revenant as animal-oid, the comic also probes questions of zoological consciousness and provokes not only terrors but also unexpected new ways to identify with the nonhuman.

Rotlanta

As Rick enters Atlanta, he has a panoramic view of a landscape where the skyline appears to hover in white light. Linear perspective gives the panel depth through the convergence of lines at a vanishing point in the distance, and the engineered vectors of the interstate offer both Rick and the reader a false sense of authority. But the horizon that blurs with outlines of hazy skyscrapers—the litter and abandoned cars—suggests that this synthetic topos, with elevated concrete expressway obscuring the contours of the terrain, is eroding as signifier. Interestingly, the panel's vanishing point is hidden by a dialogue bubble as Rick says aloud, "Here we are . . ." These words signify Atlanta's semantic and social reversibility, as its linguistic "here" acts as trace of the

Figure 2. Phantom City, *The Walking Dead*

extant city to differentiate obsolescent social constructs manifested in civil engineering and the plants and animals that still linger in city shadows. With its littered and overgrown medians—abandoned and crashed cars now at rest—both interstate and phantom city have become obscured by Rick's hollow "here." The ellipsis marks not only the human vacuum that Rick will experience downtown but also a much larger semantic fade-out along the dead interstate.

Post-apocalyptic urban migration corresponds in *The Walking Dead* to a movement out of modern history and the meaningless urban planning that made its fetish and talisman the gas-powered automobile. Expecting the city to be a place of refuge, Rick misperceives the sketchy skyline as his end point and destination. Having given up on cars—they're all on empty anyway—Rick enters the empty city on an antiquated mode of transport, a horse. But let's not think about what happens to the horse. Suffice it to say that the gory images that follow suggest that if humanity does survive, the metropolis maybe shouldn't be the very first place humans should try to start afresh. Rick will find that Atlanta—littered with hordes of starving zombies—is where his allegorical journey from the failed present to an entirely new spatial reality begins, not ends. Compendium One depicts Rick and other refugees on the road out of Atlanta as they migrate from campsite to

Figure 3. *Cathartes aura, The Walking Dead*

suburb, farm, and prison in an attempt to find a new home, and every frustrated attempt to reclaim habitat compels readers to speculate on the effects of real-world problems such as food scarcity, energy shortages, and climate-related natural disasters. So it's not entirely accurate to say that survivors in *The Walking Dead* "do not have such a clear marker of 'before' and 'after' . . . like zombies, they 'survive' in the sense of living on or beyond, but do not enter the temporal cycle where they would get to start over from scratch. They merely continue" (Pollock 175). Though it's true that a return to a pre-ecocidal condition is impossible in *The Walking Dead,* Rick and other human characters clearly desire to reenter "the temporal cycle" and start over in hopes of creating ecological *communitas* in a wild that now, as it happens, includes new species of carnivore.

Panels that depict the consumption of humans, like this close-up of a rapacious *Cathartes aura* dining on a deceased commuter, often rely on overlapping and scale to give outdoor spaces a claustrophobic air. Horizontal barriers limit vision along the failed roadway, and parallel fences separate the forest and median. Melding with the crashed car and guardrail, the angular and partially cleaned skeleton reveals its reversibility as liminal body: the skull's eye socket becomes interchangeable with the car's headlamp, and the grill conflates with the skull's teeth. This blurring of human, place, machine, and animal conjoins the turkey vulture's open eye and the human skull with the gaping hole in the car's windshield, as all three break the fourth wall. The artist's preoccupation with disturbed barriers and myopia is most apparent in the crashed car itself. If the economy sedan in this panel embodies the late-twentieth-century middle class in the United States—chugging and sputtering toward recession—any false sense of security is shattered when its human driver is flung through his windshield in an inauspicious reentry into the food chain.

Never Can Tell

"Environmental apocalypticism departs from nuclearism in that it does not posit an event at the close of history," Pollock notes in "Undead Is the New Green." The "nuclear fear promises a definitive sign—a massive explosion and iconic mushroom cloud" (174-75). In *The Walking Dead,* human death and return mean not one iconic moment or definitive end to history, but rather an accumulation of mysterious casualties and shocking events that at first manifest as solitary occurrences. Unlike nuclear holocaust, the horror of environmental apocalypse is that it is always occurring—is around us everywhere at once—and at a distance can be readily denied. Is it dead? Is it alive? Is global warming real? Is this a catastrophe? You never can tell until the thing is right up on you. So rather than being "the end," zombie apocalypse in *The Walking Dead* uses living corpses to defamiliarize both human body and place in the liminal phase so that something entirely new might arise. If the "post-nuclear zombie is the manifestation of the post-nuclear hero's greatest ontological insecurity: the loss of the 'figure' of self in his or her engulfment by the 'other'" (Boon 57), the post-ecological zombie is paradoxically the incarnation of a threatened community's greatest ontological desire: the reconfiguration of sustainable selves. Lauro and Embry's "A Zombie Manifesto" explains that in films such as the *Dawn of the Dead* remake (2004) and *28 Days Later* (2002) as well as books like Max Brooks's *The Zombie Survival Guide* (2003), the zombie "poses a twofold terror: There is the primary fear of being devoured by a zombie, a threat posed mainly to the physical body, and the second fear that one will, in losing one's consciousness, become a part of the monstrous horde" (89). But in *The Walking Dead,* as in Atwood's MaddAddam trilogy, these terrors are accompanied by an equal desire to consume cultural identity itself and protect every species of life *within* this "monstrous horde."

The Office Geek

The archetypal techie in the following panel wears a white short-sleeve button-down shirt complete with pocket protector, striped tie, steel-rimmed glasses, and black wingtips (with white socks). The clothes he wears don't appear particularly loose, so this programmer must have been pretty bony even before his death and resurrection. The fingernails have grown into claws, however, and the flesh has been removed from his skinny elbow. Our unlikely predator crouches over a white-tailed deer and has bitten into her neck, as a coyote or bear might, so that the doe can quickly bleed out. It's safe to assume that the deer was not dead when the office geek came upon it in the wilderness, but rather that he accomplished the feat of stalking and killing the animal alone. When Rick and Shane happen upon this zombie as he eats into the deer's throat, Shane wonders, "Do you think it'd be safe to eat?" This leaves the reader wondering whether zombie or deer meat might provide a more suitable dinner for the group of famished survivors, and the question as to what (or who) is food becomes key. When the office geek smells the hunters, he responds by displaying threat or anger by partially pulling back his lips, displaying bottom canines, and uttering "GRR" then the customary "RRGH!" He exhibits not only aggressive display behavior toward conspecific males but also territoriality, indicating that many animal instincts have returned for these creatures. In both the comic and TV program, Kirkman's zombies have become very much like the "scavengers, hunters and gatherers" (Newbury 90) described in Newbury's "Fast Zombie/Slow Zombie: Food Writing, Horror Movies, and Agribusiness Apocalypse." However, *The Walking Dead* makes an important lurch forward by depicting zombies and human survivors just outside the "landscape of devastated consumerism emblematized crucially by the flotsam and jetsam of corporate junk and fast food" (90), so Kirkman has moved beyond a zombie apocalypse that dismisses nature outright. Rather than offering a "world and food that are always and inescapably made by cultural and economic power" (91), *The Walking Dead* provides readers (and diners) chances to escape a fast-food Armageddon.

I disagree with Franklin Allaire's claim that zombies in *The Walking Dead* have not yet evolved to "develop communication" and that "there isn't even a hint of this happening" (202). Growling, body movements, swarming behaviors, and even pheromonal cues all indicate that these resurrected dead have developed sophisticated animal communication. Ironically, the office geek serves as a much-needed predator for white-tailed deer in the southeastern United States, and he proves to be a superb host for insects that drink from decomposed flesh and lay eggs inside rotting bodies. Romero's zombies generally ex-

Figure 4. The Office Geek, *The Walking Dead*

hibit the blank expressions of Haitian automatons even as they chase, attack, or devour humans, but the office geek has regained a level of animal vitality. Depictions of zombies stalking animal prey in the forest alter the meaning of food in this series obsessed with hunger, scarcity, foraging, and subsistence farming. Eating for the office geek is a biological need and way to sustain metabolic function, rather than some arbitrary science-fiction freak-out born of radioactive meteorites.[6] Staggering ever toward its quarry, the zombified corpse exhibits carniverous appetites and drives. Kirkman's American ghoul is motivated by the impulse to bite and guzzle available resources, exhaust the surrounding region, and then migrate out in herds and swarms to the next populous area. The eyes of zombies in *The Walking Dead* shine mirrorlike with cataracts, because the optical lenses have clouded due to rapid physical deterioration, so their mirrored eyes force survivors and readers to literally see themselves in the faces of the undead. Thus, the line between human and nonhuman animals is blurred by want of sustenance, which means that twentieth-century identity constructions in affluent nations based on delusions of unlimited resources must be shed by Rick and the other survivors as an adaptive measure. As a consequence, stable identity and nature/culture dualism are both upended to leave human beings in a liminal frontier that calls for radical new approaches to life on earth.

A Larger Skin

Post-apocalyptic narratives typically play on cultural fantasies of revolution, while the zombie tale chills its audience by holding out hope for purification and containment. In this contradictory frontier, Rick and other survivors must reconsider both the physical and psychological boundaries that separate self and territory. Undoubtedly, this realization is startling for contemporary readers who have spent their whole lives within the global hyperreal, a place where the "zombie incarnates . . . our discomfort with that boundary space that exists in us all, that objectness of our inherent material makeup whereby we transition from human to post—(as in no longer)—human" (Christie 71). This discomfort is derived from the feeling that the true self can be found only inside the brain, with both body and environs consigned to external, material "objectness." So it's important to note that in *The Walking Dead* becoming "no longer human" does not imply transcending the body's physical, emotional, and cognitive limitations to become some kind of post-object in the cloud. Rather, Kirkman's transhuman survivors must embrace an ecological identity rekindled by its very monstrosity; in the liminal zone, the definition of self "has expanded to the dimensions of the territory," because, to draw from Neil Evernden, the human creature "is no longer an organism bounded by skin—it is an organism-plus-environment bounded by an imaginary integument" (97). The larger integumentary skin Rick and his fellow migrants fashion refigures human self and physical space in the wake of infrastructure collapse. On this blurry road, humans must scavenge and kill, but they also exhibit symbiotic and altruistic behaviors because chances for individual survival are greatly increased when individuals function as herd or flock.

As Rick speaks to the group, he positions his hands in a gesture of supplication to indicate the humility of entreaty; the uniformed police officer—signifier for repressive structures—has at this stage redefined himself as equal. Rick must construct new partnerships within the group to negotiate the liminal terrain, and in so doing he undermines the subject-object split upon which the categorizations of human/zombie and human/nature are based. The movement from the top panel to the bottom, as the survivors move from road to woods, indicates a shift from asphalt highway to circle of trees as the dispersed body forms a widening ring. Now off the road, Rick and the others are distinct beings yet now part of a larger "skin" that includes not only people but also the surroundings. This skin becomes an authentic notion of selfhood for Rick's group in Compendium One. As they migrate from city to campsite, suburb, family farm, and prison, Rick and the other survivors explore the nonviability of outdated structural (and

Figure 5. Supplication, *The Walking Dead*

conceptual) frameworks to seek out future selves and social models that more effectively adjust to the limitations and dangers of their increasingly contingent lives.

Hershel's Farm

Axonometric perspectives of suburban and rural topographies drawn from satellite images and Google Maps in *The Walking Dead* incorporate a photorealism that renders humanity extrinsic to geometry. From the position of low-flying aircraft or drone, natural terrain features on Hershel's farm appear as flattened rectangles connected by an ominous blankness; this indicates synthetic replications of spatial boundaries and a loss of biodiversity. The iconic family farm, as imaged from above, enables readers to get a philosophical distance from localized agrarianism. Digital images of Hershel's farm collected by remote sensing defamiliarize the rural homestead to offer a systemic perspective that calls to question its organismal complexity and long-term viability. From this vantage point, to differentiate human habita-

Figure 6. Family Farm, *The Walking Dead*

tions from zombie lands one must identify gardening sites, as farming seems the only foolproof way to distinguish humans from the undead.

Hershel's farm provides sanctuary for Rick's band, for a while. It includes vegetable gardens, a coop filled with chickens, pastures rich with livestock . . . and a barn full of zombies. Fences once used for cow pastures now keep out stray ghouls, and makeshift partitions made from old picket fences, crossties, boards, and plywood have been constructed around the farm's perimeter. Hershel holds out hope that his dead neighbors and family members will be healed and become human again, a fundamentalist fantasy that in its naiveté fails to adapt. Dinner-table and animal-feeding rituals are designed to ward off the existential void that surrounds the farm and family, while Hershel's insistence on clinging to pre-zombie traditions and schedules leaves his family susceptible to attack. "That thing in the barn," Rick tries to explain, "it's not your son" (*WD*), which means that both the bucolic past and Hershel's conception of nature have come to an end, whether he can face it or not. Inevitably, Hershel's antiquated setup and his hold on both family and property collapse. As refugees, however, he and his kin will bring with them something far more important for the group's future: the means to grow food. It's significant that the community's garden is not grown on the family farm but behind the bars of a deserted prison. Stockpiled with canned goods, the prison has a large yard inside a series of fences where Rick plans a vegetable garden and livestock.

In one telling panel Hershel kneels with arm raised as he hammers wooden stakes into the flat ground, an allusion to the headshots and ax strikes committed during gory altercations with walking corpses. By inserting stakes in the ground, paradoxically, Hershel animates the earth by making blank spaces on the Google Map into liminal patches that will provide nourishment for self-imposed detainees who are now ravenous for fresh food. The contradictory image of Hershel and horse-drawn plow within the antiseptic prison yard makes the return of food central to Compendium One. "There's nothing quite like living off the land," Hershel says, "providing for yourself . . . knowing exactly where every piece of food you eat comes from" (*WD*). And Rick says of a garden tomato, "I don't usually eat them like this . . . you know plain, alone, like a piece of fruit . . . but these things, they're probably the best tomatoes I've ever had" (*WD*). If the ravenous mouth serves as the most important trope for reanimation in *The Walking Dead*, eating prison-grown vegetables marks the beginnings of a progressive bioregional ethos. Thus, Rick's declaration "WE ARE THE WALKING DEAD" (*WD*) becomes less an acknowledgment of the futility of the group's efforts than a recognition that *Homo sapiens* had already been culturally zombified for years before the mysterious cataclysm even occurred. Rick's statement leaves the reader wondering how long zombification had been a human condition before the viral pandemic. "This is it," Rick says in an attempt to awaken the others. "This is our life. We're not waiting here. We're not biding our time—waiting for what comes next. Or waiting to be rescued! This is what we have! This is all we'll ever have. If you want to make things better, make this place better. We have to come to grips with that" (*WD*). Stripped of his outdated identity trappings—patriarch, consumer, provider, and police—Rick can now see the prison not as a catalyst to some utopian science fiction future that will never come, but as a liminal zone that joins the conditions or "things" of human existence in "place." Eating the fresh tomato, then, means emerging from the ideological zombification of America's Frankenfood past.

Walmart of the Dead

Regrettably, Compendium One ends not with the beleaguered group working together to tend their own garden refuge, but fighting to the death with the sadistic Governor and the brainwashed minions of Woodbury. Rick, Michonne, and Glenn happen upon the small southern town of Woodbury while searching for possible survivors of a helicopter crash; they find instead refugees inside a fenced-in four-block section of town adjacent to a Walmart and National Guard post. Detained by armed townsfolk, they find that Woodbury prides itself on sporting events that feature gladiatorial cage matches with human combatants in an arena filled with chained zombies that feast upon unlucky "strangers." The sadistic Governor is propped up by a Blackwater-style citizens' militia, and he has a penchant for binding and torturing both zombies and humans Guantanamo style. Like Kaufman in *Land of the Dead*—a character based on former secretary of defense Donald Rumsfeld—the Governor maintains authority through intimidation, obfuscation, and securing multiple fences around his stronghold. He keeps animated zombie heads in aquariums, his zombie daughter Penny on a chain, and a series of labs and observation booths for his vile experiments. "I almost admire them," the Governor says of his caged zombies. "The thing you have to realize is that they're just us—they're no different. They want what they want, they take what they want and after they get what they want—they're only content for the briefest span of time. Then they want more" (*WD*). This untoward likeness between Americans and zombies—this effect of cultural claustrophobia and panopticism—Kirkman associates with Walmart. With its glaring fluorescent lights and surveillance cameras, Walmart's stark labyrinth zombifies bargain shoppers through containment corridors and the turning of towns into shopping-only turnstiles. Like the urban skyline, Woodbury's lurid and depressing commercial horizon represents a version of the past that the group must somehow get beyond to find home. When Rick, Michonne, and Glenn enter Woodbury, they describe the littered McDonald's and Walmart parking lot as utterly "dead." Black and desolate in the eerie sunset, the big-box horizon becomes as culturally meaningless as it is physically dangerous. In a subsequent panel Michonne decapitates a zombie cheerleader in the Walmart parking lot, and in another instance the dark superstore looms against an ominous sky as conditions unravel for the ragtag group. The monster is *here*, Compendium One suggests, in the superstore, the small-town mind, and the sports arena. These are places where American denial and cultural egotism hasten ecocide. Dismemberment provides an escape from this dead zone, as the gory deconstruction of the Governor's body by zombies during his siege of the prison implies a purging of the ideological and spatial frameworks upon which Walmart festers. So, yes, the future world of *The Walking Dead* is harsh, much like the twisted Paradice of Margaret Atwood's MaddAddam trilogy. In both collections one experiences a mysterious outbreak that leads to global human collapse, and there are small groups of migrants seeking new ways to survive and subsist while wild new creatures and human predators run amok. There's a dissolving

Figure 7. Big-Box Horizon, *The Walking Dead*

material infrastructure and death at every turn. But when we look to the panels' edges there are reasons to be optimistic, too. Rick and his beleaguered group now can continue their journey in hopes that the reanimated creatures that stalk them and the broken lands that still nourish them will lead to a place where they can finally let go of the past and use what they have learned, a place that just might look like the "safe and beautiful World" (*M* 385) found at the end of Atwood's *MaddAddam*.[7]

Children of Margaret

Discussing the end of *1984*, Margaret Atwood "credits Orwell's novel with grounds for 'optimism' that few readers would share" (Ingersoll 173). In "Survival in Margaret Atwood's Novel *Oryx and Crake*," Earl G. Ingersoll considers Atwood's comment that "Orwell is much more optimistic than people give him credit for. . . . Most people think the book ends when Winston comes to love Big Brother. But it doesn't. It ends with a note on Newspeak, which is written in the past tense, in standard English—which means that, at the time of writing the note, Newspeak is a thing of the past" (qtd. in Ingersoll 173). Similarly, *The Handmaid's Tale* (1985) ends with a note that reveals Gilead no longer exists, and Ingersoll suggests that the "ending of *Oryx and Crake* may be contaminated with a similar 'optimism' for which readers may have difficulty finding any firm basis" (173). Optimism in *Oryx and Crake* held little critical currency when it was first published, in part because of an initial flood of reviews and critical articles filled with apocalyptic dread. Atwood's own writings, website missives, and interviews at the time also opened the door for prescribed approaches to *Oryx and Crake*, with the Children of Margaret marking the critical territory by characterizing the first novel of the MaddAddam trilogy as a dystopian work of dark satire to be read as counterpart to *The Handmaid's Tale*.[8] But despite the obvious apocalypse, *Oryx and Crake* and the rest of the MaddAddam trilogy do indeed hold out hope for humanity and other life-forms. Like Kirkman's zombiescape, Atwood's stressed arboretum takes the reader beyond the apocalyptic moment by describing threshold creatures that mingle and merge in liminal biotopia.

Zero Hour

The first novel of Atwood's trilogy challenges readers to see forsaken lands such as Jimmy/Snowman's "Great Emptiness" (*OC* 103) not as dead and wasted spaces but as liminal zones that continue to adapt and grow, even in "zero hour" (3). As isolated survivor of Crake's genocide, Jimmy/Snowman finds himself "neither here nor there, betwixt and between all fixed points of classification" (Turner, *Dramas* 232); as an unsightly outsider, the novel's "Abominable Snowman" finds himself "existing and not existing, flickering at the edges of blizzards, apelike man or manlike ape, stealthy, elusive, known only through rumors and through its backward-pointing footprints" (*OC* 7–8). Danette DiMarco rightly observes that the Snowman's "mythic and multidirectional footprints" represent his "liminal position and potential power to repeat a past cycle of aggression against nature in the name of personal profit, or to re-imagine a way for future living grounded in a genuine concern for others" (170). When Jimmy/Snowman scrutinizes his own ecological footprint, he decides that he can no longer perpetuate the destructive methods of the past; he will embrace instead the generative capacity of places long considered doomed. The basis for hope in this first MaddAddam novel is in place, but not because, as one critic quips, the "elimination of the human race also solves the environmental crisis in one stroke" (Dunning 95). And despite the early reviews, the term *dystopian* seems appropriate to label *Oryx and Crake* only in its most generic sense, for all Orwellian social, legal, and cultural apparatus has been pretty much eliminated by the novel's first page. Jimmy/Snowman's memories could be described as contextually dystopian, as they are essentially set in the United States of the present using quasi-futuristic terminology: the "pleebland" is the depressed city, and the "compound" is the gated community or Googlesque corporate campus. This study of existent flora and fauna in the novel indicates hope for environmental reincorporation, but it is actually the "unconscionable" gene splice that requires *Oryx and Crake* to be read against the grain of critical responses that would reduce the novel to a dystopian tale that cleanly represents the author's presumed "political, social, and environmental concerns transformed into speculative fiction" (Howells, "Margaret" 161).

Early reviews of *Oryx and Crake* herald apocalyptic alarm with titles like "The End Is Nigh" (Barnacle), "Grave New World" (Gonzales), and "Bad News" (Howells). J. Brooks Bouson's article "'It's Game Over Forever'" reproaches characteristics of Jimmy's "twenty-first century world that are meant to appall us as readers" so that Atwood might draw "openly on the discourse of environmentalism [to emphasize] the effects of global warming on the future world" (142). But what does "world" actually mean to these doomsters? Discussing the uncertain ending of *Oryx and Crake*, Bouson asks, "Will it be 'game over forever', as Crake predicted? Or is there some ray of hope that humanity will survive?" (153). This choice—"game over forever" or human survival—categorically dismisses all of the flora and fauna that thrive in the novel, an oversight that is symptomatic of Atwood criticism that tries to use human-centered paradigms to wrangle with complex environmental issues. For example, Klaus Peter Müller's "Re-Constructions of Reality in Margaret Atwood's Literature: A Constructionist Approach" deduces that "there is again nothing beyond that which *human* beings have constructed, the landscape is indeed the embodied mind. That is why there is a very strong emphasis in Atwood's work on the responsibility of human beings for their constructions of landscapes, cities, and environments" (246). This sort of disjuncture between ecological crisis and literary criticism seems a missed opportunity to explore the weightier implications of Atwood's work. Clearly, what these reviews and articles leave undone in their trumpeting of generic ecological dismay is the employment of biocentric models to this biocentric novel.

One Vast Uncontrolled Experiment

Now that the trilogy has been published, it is evident that the first novel's central concern is not the end of humanity but the fate of all life. At the beginning of *Oryx and Crake*, it appears that the only person left is Jimmy/Snowman, and readers are left to dwell not on the foibles of humankind but on the "tide coming in, wave after wave sloshing over the various barricades" and the "shrieks of birds" that nest on abandoned offshore towers, with the "distant ocean grinding against the ersatz reefs of rusted car parts and jumbled bricks and assorted rubble" (*OC* 3). Two telling images resonate in this opening passage: tidal waters that erode synthetic barriers and seabirds that reign on man-made platforms. After looking at his broken watch, Jimmy/Snowman scratches his bug bites, then "scans the ground for wildlife: all quiet, no scales and tails. Left hand, right foot, right hand, left foot, he makes his way down from the tree" (4). These initial engagements with topos include flicking a spider, urinating on grasshoppers, and rubbing ants off a mango. It's clear that Jimmy/Snowman's range of vision has drastically changed because he is now a niche within an ecosystem, his primary concerns a world away from domestic and civil issues.

Most readings of *Oryx and Crake* have been species-limited in their response to a "world where everything has become altered almost beyond recognition by global warming and genetic engineering" (Howells, "*Oryx*" 170). But in "Margaret Atwood, the Land, and Ecology," published three years before *Oryx and Crake*, Ronald B. Hatch recognizes that "Atwood has something in common with recent ecocentrist writers in her rejection of the anthropomorphic viewpoint and their struggles to re-position humanity as one species among many in a web of natural connections" (181). This repositioning can be clearly seen in Jimmy/Snowman's relationship to birds and plant life in the liminal city he inhabits. He observes: "Several of the buildings once held roof gardens, and now they're top-heavy with overgrown shrubbery. Hundreds of birds streaming across the sky towards them, roostward bound. Ibis? Herons? The black ones are cormorants, he knows that for sure. They settle down into the darkening foliage, croaking and squabbling. If he ever needs guano he'll know where to find it" (*OC* 95). Buildings that once meant commerce and the towering ascendance of man have become great bird habitats, but for humans they provide only fertilizer. Jimmy/Snowman notices in another passage that a "long scrawl of birds unwinds from the empty towers—gulls, egrets, herons, heading off to fish along the shore . . . a salt marsh is forming on a one-time landfill dotted with semi-flooded townhouses. That's where all the birds are going: minnow city" (148). By returning abandoned rooftops, landfills, and townhouses to an atypical but very real "web of natural connections," these passages pursue the "theme of nature's very slow but very certain power to self-renew" (Hengen 77). In "the former park," Jimmy/Snowman observes, the "botany is thrusting itself through every crack" (*OC* 221); he imagines that it "won't be long before all visible traces of human habitation will be gone" (221–22).

This permutation, like the urban influx of birds, illustrates resilience for plant and animal life.[9] In one shattered corporate utopia called the RejoovenEsence compound, Jimmy/Snowman notes:

> Already the weeds are thick along the curbs. The street is circular; in the island in the middle, a clutch of shrubs, unpruned and scraggly, flares with red and purple flowers. Some exotic splice: in a few years they will be overwhelmed. Or else they will spread, make inroads, choke out the native plants. Who can tell which? The whole world is now one vast uncontrolled experiment—the way it always was, Crake would have said—and the doctrine of unintended consequences is in full spate. (228)

This meditation on biota and nonindigenous species is in no way speculative or futuristic; one can see this very process in any abandoned yard in the United States where exotic plants disrupt native biota. Over time, competition and adaptation will determine which indigenous and exotic species will flourish, and in *Oryx and Crake* such moments are wrought with hopeful curiosity as well as apocalyptic dread. Like it or not, the novel insists, foreign species have been introduced widely in places of concentrated human habitation, but the "uncontrolled experiment" of this landscape might well include "unintended consequences" that enable indigenous wildlife to endure.

At zero hour, Jimmy/Snowman holds out hope that his new home might one day reach a steady state with a high level of diversity for indigenous species, which would make zero not an absence without value but a reset in biological time. Jimmy/Snowman's interactions with indigenous species early in the novel also include a telling moment with a caterpillar "letting itself down on a thread" (41). This lepidopteran is "luscious, unreal green, like a gumdrop covered with tiny bright hairs"; it pauses, "smelling him, picking up on his chemical aura" (41). After noting that there "will never be another such moment of time, another such conjunction" (41), Jimmy/Snowman says to the caterpillar that both of them "have hard work to do, and loads to lift" (41). Despite the fact that Jimmy/Snowman derides himself after his caterpillar-induced "inexplicable surge of tenderness and joy" (41), the metaphor nonetheless rings true. Some caterpillar species will thrive at this end/beginning of time and "work" to make the world more complex and diverse. One cannot fail to note that like Jimmy/Snowman, the caterpillar is in a liminal stage from egg to moth or butterfly. The developmental transition of the caterpillar represents not only Jimmy/Snowman's transformation but also the mutability of the environment he inhabits.

BlyssPluss

Crake, on the other hand, has altogether abandoned binary constructions such as native/exotic, indigenous/nonindigenous, and real/fake. Crake's "scientifically advanced world no longer relies upon such oppositional logic. Within his environment the lines that separate the natural from the artificial are no longer necessary or visible" (Davis, "Natural" 89). As a scientific genius who both promotes rampant genetic modifications for corporate interests and concocts the deviously genocidal BlyssPluss pill, Crake might seem at first to serve as a corporate foil spliced together from Wells's *The Island of Dr. Moreau* and Shelley's *Frankenstein.* DiMarco figures that a "product of a profit-driven world who mirrors its economy of self-interest, Crake emerges as the quintessential *homo faber,* making it unlikely that any kind of positive social change will happen through him" (170); moreover, Crake's "scientific intelligence . . . positions him as a member of an elite class that values instrumental production only as it is linked with personal gain" (171). Ingersoll supports this contention by pointing out that Crake represents the increasing ills of the pharmaceutical industry as he "learns from and exploits corporate behavior to further his own ends" (169). Those ends, one assumes, include creating illnesses to keep "pills and profits rolling" (169). Coral Ann Howells states that "Crake the biological scientist, who espouses a purely empirical approach which devalues imagination, morality and art, appears to be an emotional blank, a state of mind imaged in his 'dark laconic clothing'" ("*Oryx*" 177). Howells also surmises that Crake's "major scientific achievements—the BlyssPluss Pill and his life work of reinventing humanity with his own genetically modified Crakers—are a mixture of vision and commercial opportunism, underpinned by an uncanny drive towards death" (178). Bouson vehemently refers to Crake as a monomaniac filled "with scientific hubris . . . who does not believe in God or Nature [and] also does not believe in the value of human life" (146). Readings such as these that blast Crake as millennial Frankenstein or corporate Moreau are incomplete because they fail to acknowledge Crake the double agent; as biohacktivist and eco-saboteur, Crake designs liminal bodies and pharmaceuticals to reveal a paradoxical yearning for ecological utopia in a world—to paraphrase Turner—that will little resemble its past or present state.

Crake's most telling literary progenitor is not Victor Frankenstein, who has "drunk also of the intoxicating draught" (Shelley 29) of scientist hubris, but rather Gore Vidal's Kalki, a religious idol turned ecosaboteur who renders the human race extinct with lotuses laced with a global dose of the deadly bacterium *Yersinia enterocolitica.* As covert multinational Luddite, Crake fabricates a cover story to orchestrate worldwide human extermination so that the posthuman Children of Crake and the remaining extant life on earth might endure. As clock-stopping initiator of zero hour and the Waterless Flood, Crake's creations might be "seen less as a border or a limit between two already constituted worlds than as a space-time gap . . . through which a new world gradually emerges or is brought into being" (Spariosu 118). For good or ill, Crake's customized world is obviously generated by his advanced understanding of nature and its fragility. He explains the paradox of human carrying capacity to Jimmy by asking him to "look at it realistically. You can't couple a minimum access to food with an expanding population indefinitely. *Homo sapiens* doesn't seem able to cut himself off at the supply end. He's one of the few species that doesn't limit reproduction in the face of dwindling resources" (*OC* 119–20). Crake describes the effects of the BlyssPluss pill in reproductive terms and declares that his pharmaceutical will "eliminate the external causes of death" such as "[o]verpopulation, leading—as we've seen in spades—to environmental degradation and poor nutrition" (293). In both passages, Crake dispassionately explains what will invariably happen to existing resources, clean air, and water if global human population numbers continue to double at the current rate. "Demand for resources," Crake reminds us, "has exceeded supply for decades in marginal geopolitical areas, hence the famines and droughts; but very soon, demand is going to exceed supply *for everyone*" (295). Ignoring the social implications of his own assessment, Crake obliges readers to consider the long-term effects of rapid human population increase on a global scale. In so doing, the novel gives rise to a number of hard questions: What happens to customary human qualities associated with the Western post-industrial state in a world with housing and energy shortages, starvation, and drought? What happens to the inviolability of a human populace that lacks the resources to lobby for its own aims? What does it mean to be human when one's only goal, day after day, is to keep from dying?

Clearly influenced by Richard Matheson's *I Am Legend* (1954), *Oryx and Crake* modifies the dynamic between last man and group of post-apocalyptic creatures because—unlike vampires or zombies—Crakers pose no threat to Atwood's Omega Man. Crakers instead serve as metonymic "floor models" (302) in the trilogy to promote alternative versions of humanity within millennial contexts, not in *arrière-garde* outrage but to provoke philosophical speculations that are far more unsettling. Designed in a high-security dome compound, Paradice, Crake's "environmentally friendly hominids" (Bouson 141) are depicted not as grotesque but as having supra-human beauty. Upon first seeing the Crakers, Jimmy "couldn't believe them, they were so beautiful. Black, yellow, white, brown, all available skin colors. Each individual was exquisite" (*OC* 302). Crake masters genetic engineering technologies to design human-ish creatures with not only aesthetic appeal but also resistance to climate change, insects, militarism, and starvation. In regard to sexual reproduction, Ingersoll succinctly explains: the "female goes into heat about every three years, cueing the males through the release of the appropriate pheromones, accompanied by visual signals of her readiness to mate: her genitalia and the adjacent area turn blue, an adaptation Crake copied from other higher primates" (168). To ensure fertility, the "mating ritual requires that three males copulate with the female in turn, following a courting dance in which they woo her by waving their erect penises that have turned blue to mark their readiness to mate" (168). Critics have emphasized satirical aspects of the Crakers to include their dining and sexual proclivities, and some feel that it's "hard to take these purring, multi-colored, blue-bottomed, blue-penised, excrement-eating, perimeter-pissing, citrous-scented creatures seriously" (Dunning 95). But when we observe these very traits in other animal species, they are understood as appropriate to specific adaptive functions. From the "ancient primate brain" are taken "its destructive features, the features responsible for the world's current illnesses. For instance, racism—or, as they referred to it in Paradice, pseudospeciation—had been eliminated in the model group, merely by switching the bonding mechanism: the Paradice people simply did not register skin colour" (*OC* 305). Also, hierarchical thinking "could not exist among them," Crake explains, and "there was no territoriality"; they "ate nothing but leaves and grass and roots and a berry or two; thus their foods were plentiful and always available" (305). Regarding the Crakers as metaphors for human degradation, Ingersoll asks that if "life can survive only in the form of the Children of Crake, doesn't that survival outweigh the loss of some of what readers are likely to consider their 'humanity'? No, in thunder! Atwood seems to be shouting. If traditional human qualities have to be sacrificed in order to survive, it may not be worth surviving" (Ingersoll 167). Problems of authorial intent aside, it's clear that life and humanity appear to be surviving in increasingly diverse forms in *Oryx and Crake* as they slowly adapt to new topographies left by human cataclysm. Ecocritically, the question of readers' "humanity" and "traditional human qualities" in opposition to survival seems secondary to these questions: What is the relationship of these life-forms to their bioregion? What do the Crakers teach us about our own biotic relationships?

Crakers embody genetically what Atwood's millennial readers might aspire to behaviorally, and thus part of the novel's optimism can be found in the hope that western culture might over time become a little more Craker-like. Programmed to respect all species of life, Crakers don't fight, don't waste, and they know how to share. Jimmy/Snowman thinks after stepping on a banana slug that "if he were a Craker he'd have to apologize to it—*I'm sorry I stepped on you, Child of Oryx, please forgive my clumsiness*" (*OC* 334). Even the troublesome dining habits of the Crakers prompt ecocritical readers to reconsider issues of waste in a book preoccupied with food security, garbage, and the politics of excrement. Lastly, Crakers also help us to remember that humans aren't exempted from adaptations and mutations that occur through processes of evolution, despite our big brains. Before his death Crake compels readers to remember that as liminal creatures ourselves in passage among multiple states of being, *Homo sapiens* has the capacity over time to shed the genetic basis for attributes that lead to war and ecocide. Thus, essentialist conceptions of human inviolability that many Atwood critics have championed are cunningly spliced by the author with monstrosities of corporate science to remanufacture traditional philosophical categories of authentic, synthetic, and real. Just as Oryx explains that all "sex is real" (144), cosmetic surgery mishaps, cloning, predation by GM animals, and urban starvation are also real regardless of where and how they originated. If it can hurt you, the novel suggests, it's real.

Splice Genius

Before the BlyssPluss pill is introduced, depictions of animal-based transgenic hybrids are often described with as much humor as horror, and Atwood's animal genetic materials sometimes characterize abuses by multinational food and pharmaceutical conglomerates with a cloying lightness.[10] The stylistic playfulness of terms such as "ChickieNobs Bucket O' Nubbins" (7) and "Organ-Oink Farms" (22) threatens to gloss over depictions of real corporate slaughterhouses and synthetic food labs. Moreover, Atwood's novel appears to delight in depicting MaddAddam bioform resistance organisms such as pox-infected wasps that annihilate ChickieNobs, car-destroying rodents "containing elements of both porcupine and beaver" (217), and a microbe that eats "tar and asphalt" that "had turned several interstate highways into sand" (217). But, in the end, even these threshold bodies serve to resist their corporate makers. Crake briefly mentions the covert MaddAddam "splice geniuses," describing them as saboteurs who are "after the whole system" and "want to shut it down" (217). Crake's biological cosmology offers much more than a modest proposal for contemporary humanity because it develops a guide for negotiating and surviving cyborg landscapes and life-forms to come. As a Crusoe figure who "goes animal" within a shifting ecosystem, Jimmy/Snowman will offer leadership and engender hope in the face of crisis. He, like Rick in *The Walking Dead*, must now reconstitute identity in liminality and conceive ecological *communitas* through solitary survival, a return to the source of trauma, and renegotiation with the monstrous. "Last man" no longer, he must consider cultural and spiritual responses to his new ecological context, a quandary taken up by the God's Gardeners in *The Year of the Flood* and *MaddAddam*. An ecocritical reading of flora and fauna in *Oryx and Crake* suggests that Jimmy/Snowman's pilgrimage of confused identity, outsiderhood, ecological apprehension, and obligation will invariably end in bioregional utopia. His predicament at the end of the novel reflects our own dilemma at this crossroads in environmental history "when everything, as it were, trembles in the balance" (Turner, *Ritual* 44).

Serpent Wisdom

The dizzying second novel in the trilogy, set in the same area and time period as *Oryx and Crake*, focuses on women's experiences both in and out of the "exfernal world" by highlighting the struggles of two female protagonists contained within CorpSeCorps structures during and after the BlyssPluss genocide. In *The Year of the Flood*, God's Gardener Toby is stuck inside an AnooYoo spa at the same time that her friend Ren—a trapeze artist at zoological strip club Scales and Tails—is quarantined inside a "Sticky Zone" holding cell. If, as Hannes Bergthaller explains, "sexual violence against women and children is Atwood's most important trope for the general breakdown of cultural restraints" (Bergthaller 733), then sexual predation and trafficking of young women in *The Year of the Flood* is a key trope for environmental breakdown as well. It follows that the portentous convergence of women and nonhuman life before the Waterless Flood is meant to relegate both to the status of hybridized prey. As an adolescent, Ren sees posters at the entrance to Scales and Tails of "beautiful girls covered completely with shining green scales, like lizards, except for the hair. One of them was standing on a single leg with the other leg hooked around her neck. I thought it must hurt to stand like that, but the girl in the picture was smiling" (*YF* 74). Girls in the "snake pit" become reptilian in Atwood's corporate ghetto, making both wildlife and women tantamount to game for Blanco and other would-be hunters; the sexualization of endangered animal species becomes interchangeable with liminal women who have been degraded by poverty and abuse. The lizard woman on the poster is a contortionist, smiling with her leg behind her head, which implies that Atwood's pre-apocalyptic dystopia disfigures both woman and animal in carnival performance to satisfy the urges of human creatures with atrophied abilities to pair-bond outside of abusive exchange models.

Painballers and others who patronize this pleebland club are aroused in the same way that men of the higher classes become excited by furzooters, as Toby learns when she takes a job working the "higher-end malls and the boutique retail streets" (31). Furzooters are day laborers who "put on fake-fur animal suits with cartoon heads and [hang] advertising signs around their necks" (31), and Toby recalls being attacked on more than one occasion by frantic plushophiles who sometimes "knocked her over, twisted the big head around so she was blinded, and rubbed their pelvises against her fur, making strange noises, of which the meows were the most recognizable" (31). The animal-human hybridity motif in *Oryx and Crake* takes another bizarre yet important philosophical turn in *The Year of the Flood,* because it confuses and conflates organ trafficking with the sex trade, as caged pigoons fashioned with human neocortex are replaced by contained women who masquerade in animal skins. The placement of female bodies into fur suits and scaly Biofilm Bodygloves implies that environmental upheaval in this novel has generated a sideshow of in-between creatures that displace and distort yearnings for some sort of harmonious relationship with other species and the landscape. In this curious psychological state, wealthy people in the compounds "overloaded with expensive skin" wear "alligator slingbacks, leopard minis, [and] oryx-hide handbags" (142). In all of these cases, totemic animals are fetishized to imitate and prostitute liminal bodies.

Toby and Ren undergo similar transformations throughout the book as both women transition from troubled families to the God's Gardeners cult to the nefarious CorpSeCorps. The AnooYoo spa where Toby is fortified at the beginning of the novel is described as a place to "get yourself resurfaced" (116), where women can buy cosmetics such as "AnooYoo Luscious Polish," "AnooYoo Plum Skin Plumper," and "AnooYoo Fountain of Youth Total Immersion" so they can "*Shed That Scaly Epidermis!*" (237). Meditating on products that have become meaningless since the Waterless Flood, Toby muses, "I could have a whole new me [. . .]. Yet another whole new me, fresh as a snake" (237). Shedding, snake, and scale images throughout the novel link upscale beauty salon AnooYoo, HelthWyzer, and swanky strip club Scales and Tails as interworking facets of a unified operation designed to demoralize then market mutable women by continually removing and replacing their skins. But the snake woman also becomes an important motif in *The Year of the Flood* because it reveals in the shedding of skin a molting of feminine identity that will take place when Toby/Tobiatha and Ren escape from their prisons. As threshold beings in worldwide collapse, these women become limen when their psychological and morphological conversions upend the logic of AnooYoo. As snake women, they have the chance to attain what Adam One calls the "importance of instinctive knowing" (*YF* 233), or Serpent Wisdom, which is described as the "wisdom of *feeling directly*, as the Serpent feels vibrations in the Earth" (234). Atwood's snake women are sensitive to these ethical "vibrations" and grow intuitive, sly, and streetwise enough to protect themselves against a host of predators. We learn in *MaddAddam* that when Zeb disguises himself as a Scales and Tails bouncer, Adam One gives him an "enameled lapel pin in the shape of a snake eating its own tail," which he explains is "an ancient motif that meant regeneration" (*M* 294). Therefore, the capture and release of serpentine women parallels not only the exodus of genetically modified wildlife such as liobams and Mo'Hairs but also bioforms such as the "microbes that [eat] asphalt" and "mice that [attack] cars" (*YF* 333). Like hybridized wildlife these transitional figures become outsiders who threaten the CorpSeCorps monopoly.

What Can't Be Mended

Despite their many eccentricities and flaws,[11] the last best chance for ecological harmony in *The Year of the Flood* can be found in the God's Gardeners, a cult that fosters a strict ethos of stewardship at a time described as otherwise "suffering from the results of an ultimately deadly, reckless experimentation with biotechnology, coupled with a widespread social lack of any investment or belief in sustainability, ecological balance or natural harmonious existence" (Wisker 176). As espoused by Adam One, Gardener philosophy promotes a survivalist ethos that sermonizes on the errors of primate humanity since the "fall" from our arboreal beginnings, rebuilding a sacred trust with other life-forms, vegetarianism, reusing waste, foraging, and composting. Central to the Gardener creed is the disavowal of mass-produced pharmaceuticals, telecommunications, and foods. It is also assumed that Adam One harbors a "dream of restoring all the lost Species via their preserved DNA codes, once a more ethical and technically proficient future had replaced the depressing present" (*YF* 247). As part of an underground resistance movement, Adam One and other Gardeners are also involved in clandestine acts of corporate espionage, hacking, sabotage, and identity theft. The Gardeners train for end times and live austere lifestyles to acquire the survivalist training and spiritual grounding needed to make it through the prophesied Waterless Flood.

Bergthaller sees in Gardener practice, more than cultist indoctrination, "insight behind the handicrafts, the gardening, the liturgical calendar, and all the other ritualized activities around which the Gardeners' communal life is organized," because their sustainable practices "impart useful ecological knowledge and habitualize the group's members to environmentally responsible behavior" (740). It's important to note that the two most important rituals of Gardener life practice are foraging and composting. Burt's lesson on Wild Botanicals focuses on what might "happen if suddenly there were no more supermarkettes" (*YF* 149), and Adam One praises "Saint" Euell Gibbons, who "sang the virtues of the wild Onion, of the wild Asparagus, of the wild Garlic," who "taught us not to waste" but "to improvise" (126). Adam One preaches that "if there is no Sorrel, there may be Cattails; and if there are no Blueberries, the wild Cranberry may perhaps abound" (126). Wild medicinal herbs as well as animals such as bees and flesh-eating maggots help the rooftop garden prosper. The Gardeners offer an alternative vision of the external world that allows for life in death, nourishment in waste, and resurrected ghettoes among the dying pleebs. "What can't be mended may still be tended" (279) is an important mantra for the Gardeners, because foraged food and composted materials sustain the cult while also undermining the CorpSeCorps cartel. At the time of her death, for example, Pilar has her body planted in the public park, because in Gardener philosophy she is "donating herself to the matrix of Life through her own volition" (179). Gardeners compost rather than bury their dead, and Pilar is interred with an elderberry shrub planted on top of her so that the Gardeners might get "some foraging dividends" (183). Adam One preaches the Gardener gospel because, in his words, the "Waterless Flood is coming, in which all buying and selling will cease, and we will find ourselves thrown back upon our own resources, in the midst of God's bounteous Garden" (126).

Environmental Eugenics?

This brings us to perhaps the most controversial issue in the MaddAddam trilogy: the link between global genocide and utopian fantasy. Unlike Rachel Stein, I do not find Adam One a satirical figure when he makes such arguments as "We have betrayed the trust of the Animals, and defiled our sacred task of stewardship. God's commandment to 'replenish the Earth' did not mean we should fill it to overflowing with ourselves, thus wiping out everything else" (52–53). Adam One approaches issues of human population and biodiversity from a data-driven perspective that overlooks reproductive rights, patriarchal abuses, and other social-justice concerns. Similarly, Toby/Tobiatha states to the Crakers in *MaddAddam* that either most humans "must be cleared away while there is still an earth, with trees and flowers and birds and fish and so on, or all must die when there are none of these things left. Because if there are none of these things left, then there will be nothing at all. Not even any people" (*M* 291). There's no question that many Gardeners, like Crake, adhere to a conceptual framework wherein cultural and economic interests become secondary to problems of species extinction, biodiversity, clean water and air, conservation, and global sustainability. And though claims made by Adam One and many zero population growth advocates upon whom his argument is based are overly simplistic, to disregard human population dynamics as a most important factor in the world's environmental conundrum is to turn a blind eye to a central challenge that Atwood explicitly addresses again and again throughout the trilogy.

In "Sex, Population, and Environmental Eugenics in Margaret Atwood's *Oryx and Crake* and *The Year of the Flood*," Stein argues that by "targeting sex/reproduction and universally condemning human presence instead of our destructive social behaviors, such as corporate, capitalist consumption and scientific commodification—eugenic environmentalism makes the fatal assumption that human nature cannot possibly co-exist with non-human nature, that we cannot reform our social/economic modes of life in order to live sustainably, and that the only way to save earth is to destroy *Homo sapiens*" (197–98). If we were to follow Stein's contention to the trilogy's unflinchingly utopian denouement, the entire series would be discredited as "eugenic environmentalism." I do not take such a view, because it obscures Atwood's point about western culture's blinding destruction of the nonhuman that precipitates humanity's collapse. Rather than endorsing a neo-eugenicist "Earth or *Homo sapiens*" binary, Atwood's novels honor biotic and human communities of all shapes and sizes, offer no-nonsense ideas for promoting quality of human life, and also expose habits and practices that contribute to our current crisis. By constructing figures and spaces that adapt through natural selection and bioengineering to reach *communitas,* Atwood also imagines many second chances for both humanity and posthumanity. Atwood's posthuman vision shares much with the work of Sherryl Vint, who argues in *Bodies of Tomorrow* (2007) that the

> "post" of posthumanism should not be a post-biological embodiment. The "post" of posthumanism should be a "post" to the heritage of humanism, which makes humans the only subjects in a world of objects. An ethical posthumanism must work against this boundary of the human from the nonhuman, refusing this final ground of abjection. An ethical posthumanism which acknowledges that self is materially connected to the rest of the world, in affinity with its other subjects, is an accountable posthumanism. (189)[12]

Crake's use of genetic engineering to reshape natural selection in *MaddAddam* also ultimately serves to delete the "grinning, elemental malice" (*M* 41) found in "old biblical kings" (40), male "alpha-chimp display"

(298), and the impulse to pair-bond in marriage. Atwood associates "the chaos"—the world of the twenty-first-century reader and the MaddAddamites' recent past—with masculine violence. By assassinating the captured painballers at the end of *MaddAddam*—they are "cleared away" (358) as a final stage of Crake's vision—the coalition of MaddAddamites, Gardeners, pigoons, and Crakers essentially free themselves from what amounts to high testosterone levels. But if we look closely at the environmental and gender dynamics at the end of the trilogy, it would be as ill advised to consider Atwood's work "eugenic feminism" as it would be to deem it "eugenic environmentalism," if only because the traditional means of transmitting human genetic material in the new utopia becomes an outmoded and meaningless trope.[13] Toby/Tobiatha reminds readers in *MaddAddam* that despite all of the collective horror found in the trilogy, it's "not the end of the world" (205), which means that if readers get too caught up in the abortive past, they might miss the crucial point about how environmental communities are born.

Reboot

Expanding Jimmy/Snowman's genesis myth, Toby/Tobiatha tells the Crakers that "all around the Egg was the chaos, with many, many people who were not like you . . . many of them were bad people who did cruel and hurtful things to one another, and also to the animals" (3). She pronounces that the "people in the chaos cannot learn. They cannot understand what they are doing to the sea and the sky and the plants and the animals" (291). But inside the egg of Paradice, Oryx lays two smaller eggs, one "full of animals and birds and fish" that includes not only butterflies, snakes, and frogs but also transgenic "rakunks, and bobkittens, and Mo'Hairs, and Pigoons" (289–90). Rather than create a "perfect world," Zeb explains, Crake has granted the planet a "reboot" (334) where indigenous plants and animals compete with invasive species and genetically modified organisms. Both *The Year of the Flood* and *MaddAddam* fixate on the role of marginal and undervalued life-forms such as vultures, maggots, bees, and even kudzu as species that fill important roles in Atwood's phantom zone. "*Vultures are our friends,*" Toby/Tobiatha recalls from the Gardeners. "*They purify the earth. They are God's necessary dark Angels of bodily dissolution*" (*YF* 3). One Gardener hymn even describes God as a vulture who "Death does eat, corruption too, / And thus does Life restore" (373). And in a pinch, all good Gardeners know, maggots can be tasty "land shrimp" (328) or "helpful creatures" who heal rotting human bodies because they not only "eat the decaying flesh, they [kill] necrotic bacteria, and [are] thus a great help in preventing gangrene" (108). Bees, which "all over the world had been in trouble for decades" (100),[14] appear in *MaddAddam* to be gaining in numbers, but the same can be said for nonindigenous kudzu "clambering up the walls" (377) and "covering the broken shapes" of exfernal detritus "with a soft fledging of green" (347). "Aggressive kudzu" provides food for not only the Crakers and Mo'Hairs but also humans, whose post-Armageddon diet plan now includes such culinary delights as kudzu spinach-style and kudzu pancakes. Toby/Tobiatha feels there "would be no point in being a Gardener now," after the Waterless Flood, because the "enemies of God's Natural Creation no longer exist, and the animals and birds—those that did not become extinct under the human domination of the planet—are thriving unchecked. Not to mention the plant life" (*M* 209). Rigid Gardener ideology has been replaced in the wake of the "Great Rearrangement" (289) by a community of mutual survival.

So it's not surprising that pollination, procreation, and birth are predominant tropes at the trilogy's conclusion. Even at the end of *The Year of the Flood*, Gardeners begin to observe the first signs of reanimation in the rearranged planet left after the Waterless Flood; Adam One tells his flock "how privileged we are to witness these first precious moments of Rebirth! How much clearer the air is, now that man-made pollution has ceased! The freshly cleansed air is to our lungs as the air up there in the clouds is to the lungs of Birds. . . . Even now, my Friends, the rainforest must be regenerating!" (*YF* 371–72). The dialectic of cleansing and regeneration is employed to describe the planet's slow movement from liminality to *communitas*. "Here comes the sun," Toby/Tobiatha observes, "a hot rose lifting out of peach-coloured clouds. The leaves on the overhanging trees are covered with tiny droplets that shine in the strengthening pink light. Everything looks so fresh, as if newly created" (383). Edenic undertones and Beatles riffs are used to describe the regenesis of a bioregion in a world thought doomed. Adam One explains that "humans must labour to believe, as the other Creatures do not. They know the dawn will come. They can sense it—that ruffling of the half-light, the horizon bestirring itself" (235). Dawn does come in *MaddAddam*, though Adam One and his Gardener ethos do not survive to see it. Amanda, Ren, and Swift Fox not only live to see it but are all impregnated by the Crakers to produce live births, signifying to Blackbeard and the entire community that Crakers, Gardeners, and MaddAddamites alike "are all people and helpers, though we have different gifts" (*M* 386). The novel ends with Blackbeard's "Book," which contains "the Words of Crake, and the Words of Oryx as well, and of how together they made us, and made also this safe and beautiful World for us to live in" (385). The irony of Crake becoming a deity alongside divine environmentalists such as Saint Rachel Carson and Saint E. O. Wilson is lost on the Crakers, who will chronicle the planet's dark rite of passage through liminality to biotopia as scripture.

This Is (Not) the End

Victor Turner explains that when a person "ceases to be the master and becomes the equal or fellow" of other humans, that person "also ceases to be master and becomes the equal or fellow of nonhuman beings. It is culture that fabricates structural distinctions; it is culture too that eradicates these distinctions in liminality" (Turner, *Dramas* 252-53). Like *The Walking Dead,* Atwood's trilogy reveals not "The End" but a literary and cultural yearning for a new start—an ecological *communitas* remade from a world where cultural distinctions and borders have generated "more plagues, more famines, more floods, more insect or microbe or small-mammal outbreaks, more droughts, more chickenshit boy-soldier wars in distant countries" (*OC* 253-54). More than simply rehearsing disaster, Atwood's novels attempt—with more optimism than she is given credit for—to see through apocalypse beyond a warming world where, we are told, "everything was being ruined and would never be the same again" (63). Though the works studied in this book neither condone nor accept ecocidal acts, they offer much more than despair in the face of damage done. Atwood's liminal world inspires us to use Gardener biocentricity, MaddAddamite knowledge, and Craker understanding to reanimate and tend our living earth.

Coda

When studied together, the literary works in these chapters offer a profound eco-political message for our future. First and foremost, we have to recognize that the drive for purity in the liminal zone is the drive to despair. There's no going back now. What is called for instead is acceptance, not surrender to ecological destruction or social injustice but an enlightened acceptance of greatly disturbed landscapes in the Western Hemisphere as they now stand. This approach will create room for imaginative possibilities that can never be realized by clinging to the past. Second, these books encourage for liminal communities a healthy skepticism of globalization and the technologies of empire. They advocate instead a localist ethos that fosters small-scale democracy, urban revival, sustainable agriculture, population balance, and climate consciousness. Third, these works urge communities to remap habitats to honor local food, regional craft, traditional methods, and even waste. Suspicious of the borders and fences that define our contemporary lives, these authors know that the walls maintaining antiquated categorizations such as culture/nature, male/female, and white/nonwhite are quickly losing their meaning. Finally, they challenge readers to rethink the biological order that has historically defined western life and livelihood. Against speciesism, these works allow for the empathic merging of *Homo sapiens* and other forms of life and, in many cases, support animal rights.

In the introduction I asked what *communitas* in the Western Hemisphere might look like, and from these chapters a few patterns emerge that provide a partial answer. Perhaps most importantly, we need to think of the Western Hemisphere not in its decrepitude but in a sort of protracted adolescence. Our pubescent New World is at the moment an emotional wreck. It's experimenting with all kinds of destructive habits and styles, developing in all sorts of confusing ways, and is hard to control. But it's just a phase, just a stage we're going through. Maturity will come, and with it experience and wisdom. Will our juvenile-delinquent nations need to hit rock bottom before getting it together?

The authors studied in this book think not. But it is clear that *communitas* can begin in earnest only when individuals and households get a grip on their own domestic lives, which means for one thing getting cheap. Interest slavery, the fetish of the new and shiny, and the crisis of our disposable culture all work hand-in-hand to create a choleric, self-involved, and overworked populace. Environmental enlightenment can't come from minds like that! The millennial family will benefit from remembering that stocks are not only abstract lines on TV but can also be stores of canned produce in the pantry. People fortunate enough to own yards and have a good water supply might try to grow 10 percent of their own food. Ornamental trees, bushes, and plant life can be replaced by aesthetically appealing alternatives that bear fruit, nuts, vegetables, and herbs. The manicured, poisoned, and irrigated lawn has got to go and can be replaced by monster yards that luxuriate with indigenous life, livestock, flowering weeds, and plenty to forage. Threadbare duds, clunky cars, mismatched furniture, dog-eared library books, well-tuned bikes, and public transport cards all comprise this scruffy utopia.

As far as cuisine is concerned, foodies of the future will eat more like the urban rich or the agrarian poor because they will understand that when it comes to seasonal food these two groups have quite a few things in common. Both take advantage of fresh, local fruits and vegetables because they are much tastier and quite often less expensive than the packaged, wilted counterfeits in the supermarket. Millennial eaters will explore roadside stands, bent-and-dent stores, U-picks, and CSAs. They'll learn about gardening, canning, freezing, hunting, fishing, and foraging. Carnivores, let's not be hypocritical about this. Killing, cleaning, and cooking animals yourself make what ends up on the plate less of an abstraction. Getting meat exclusively at the market or restaurant is a privilege that can be better appreciated when one experiences hunting and gathering firsthand. Tastier, and quite often cheaper, food closer to the source liberates consumers from the shiny boxes, plastic wraps, corn oil, salt, and artery-clogging gunk associated with the middle of the grocery store, the drive-thru, and the tasteless single-serving "convenience" of the middle-class grind.

On a municipal level, *communitas* will come from the resources, structures, idiosyncrasies, and opportunities of specific regions. There's no one-size-fits-all in bioregional community building. Growth will need to become centripetal, however, which means developers will need incentives to turn back inward toward the center rather than expanding in the old way. Preexisting structures of all sorts in centripetal spaces can be reused as homes, stores, libraries, and civic centers, as communities retrofit to honor and enhance what's already there. And this work is already happening. Forward-thinking townships, municipalities, cities, and rural enclaves all over the globe are coming up with grassroots models for improving walkability, local trade, housing, water conservation, creative zoning, and sustainability. Our new community will have the bikeways of Minneapolis, the public transit system of Vancouver, and the walkability of New York. Tucson will be our model for rainwater harvesting, and we'll adopt the zero-waste strategy of Oakland. The wind energy of La Ventosa and the solar energy plan of northern Chile will guide our power infrastructure, and initiatives such as Sunshine Community Gardens in Austin and the Rooftop Garden Project in Montreal offer examples of excellence in localized food production. As for farmer's markets, the Chattanooga Market in Tennessee and the Mercado de Rio Piedras in Puerto Rico will be our primary sources of inspiration, and in terms of low-cost housing we'll follow the precedent set by Auburn University's Rural Studio. Virtually all of these successes began on the grassroots level and are profound examples of what the future could look like. Put these elements together and you're getting close to *communitas* in towns, cities, and rural communities as livable as Calgary, Portland, or Curitiba. Waiting for sublime global miracles or spectacular media disasters will only lead to depression. But creating a little miracle, that's *communitas.*

Notes

Introduction

1. Regarding the psychological effects of the atomic bomb, Buell writes in *Writing for an Endangered World*, "Love Canal, Three Mile Island, Bhopal, Chernobyl, the *Exxon Valdez*: this modern mantra refers both to actual incidents and to events in the history of postindustrial imagination that ensured that the environmental apocalypticism activated by Hiroshima and Nagasaki would outlast the Cold War" (Buell, *Writing* 32).

2. See Dillon and Lavender.

3. Texts germane to this discussion include Higonnet's *Borderwork: Feminist Engagements with Comparative Literature* (1994); Henderson's *Borders, Boundaries, and Frames: Essays in Cultural Criticism and Cultural Studies* (1995); Inness and Royer's *Breaking Boundaries: New Perspectives on Women's Regional Writing* (1997); Warren and Dickie's *Challenging Boundaries: Gender and Periodization* (2000); and Norquay and Smyth's *Across the Margins: Cultural Identity and Change in the Atlantic Archipelago* (2002).

4. Margulis and Hird offer biocentric models and alternative ways to conceptualize both self and community within ecological networks. See also Roughgarden. Kaplan and Rogers's *Gene Worship* moves this conversation in compelling directions as well.

5. From Turner's *Dramas, Fields, and Metaphors: Symbolic Action in Human Society*: "The first stage, separation, comprises symbolic behavior signifying the detachment of the individual or the group from either an earlier fixed point in the social structure or from an established set of cultural conditions (a 'state'). During the intervening liminal period, the state of the ritual subject (the 'passenger' or 'liminar,') becomes ambiguous, neither here nor there, betwixt and between all fixed points of classification; he passes through a symbolic domain that has few or none of the attributes of his past or coming state. In the third phase the passage is consummated and the ritual subject . . . reenters the social structure" (Turner, *Dramas* 232).

6. See Shutkin and Mares.

7. Huggan and Tiffin's *Postcolonial Ecocriticism* (2010) develops key connections between colonialism and depletionism and includes an intriguing description of "zoocriticism." See also Roos and Hunt.

8. Mainstream American culture has also been undergoing the "great and

necessary advance" of seeking to reuse "urban and other severely altered, damaged landscapes" (Buell, *Future* 88) for green ventures ranging from urban farming to city planning. Recent examples from the flood of nonfiction guides for spatial reanimation include such titles as *Breaking through Concrete: Building an Urban Farm Revival* (2012) and *Urban Homesteading: Heirloom Skills for Sustainable Living* (2011); propositions for green-minded advances in design can be found in *Green Infrastructure: A Landscape Approach* (2013) and *The Upcycle: Beyond Sustainability, Designing for Abundance* (2013). Edward Humes's book *Garbology: Our Dirty Love Affair with Trash* (2012) tantalizes audiences by poking around the trash industry and proposing smart ways to deal with our mountainous landfills and unsightly waste.

9. Of course the scholarly deconstruction of Nature has been under way for decades. See Leo Marx's *Machine in the Garden* (1964), for example, or Michael A. Bryson's *Visions of the Land* (2002), which suggests that by "critically evaluating the many ways nature has been seen through the eyes of science, we can move beyond limiting models of nature, whether gendered or mechanistic, which define the environment as mere resource . . . and imagine an environmentally engaged scientific outlook based not upon the desire to control and reshape the earth but upon the goal of restoring health and equity to our relationship with nature" (179–80).

Chapter 1

1. Struebig touches upon this issue in "Nature and Sexuality in Gabriel García Márquez's *One Hundred Years of Solitude*."

2. Central to this discussion is Bell-Villada's "Banana Strike and Military Massacre: *One Hundred Years of Solitude* and What Happened in 1928." See also Posada-Carbó.

3. A lucid description of the Ciénaga massacre can be found in Palacios 83–85.

4. In "The Role of Climate in Twentieth-Century Spanish American Fiction," McMurray links climate to "hyperbole and comedy" (64).

5. Geographer Gary S. Elbow writes a thorough meteorological assessment of the Aracataca region in "Creating an Atmosphere: Depiction of Climate in the Works of Gabriel García Márquez."

6. A superb overview and ecocritical survey of *Tropic of Orange* can be found in Gamber 120–54. Time didn't stand still when Hurricane Katrina devastated New Orleans, any more than when Hurricane San Calixto II ravaged the Lesser Antilles in 1780.

7. For a primer on Mesoamerican snake and jaguar myths, start with Read and González.

Chapter 2

1. In *Drawing the Line* (2001), Danson delves into the science and logistics behind the surveyors' achievement in a most useful accompanying text for readers of *Mason & Dixon*.

2. The "grandest" of the North American effigy mounds is the "depiction

of an undulating snake, perhaps a stylized rattlesnake, in Adams County, Ohio, known as the Great Serpent Mound. Over 1,300 feet long, with an average height of four to five feet and a width of 20 to 25 feet, the serpent is located on a wedge-shaped, slightly convex ridge in the rolling hills of southern Ohio where it overlooks a waterway called Brush Creek. . . . The exact function of the great mount, within the clay structure of which no culturally identifiable objects have yet been located, is uncertain" ("Great Serpent Mound").

3. England's fifth Astronomer Royal, Nevil Maskelyne, attempted in 1761 to observe the transit of Venus on the island of St. Helena but was disappointed by clouds. See Howse.

4. Invasive aquatic species in the United States are discussed in Leland 162–65, 187–99.

5. The complicated history of this dispute is summarized in "Historical Prelude to the Survey of Mason and Dixon" in *The Journal of Charles Mason and Jeremiah Dixon* (1969).

6. Frontiersman Captain Evan Shelby is described as "a somewhat dubious character" (Danson 133). See Danson 144–46.

7. A guide who in his head "carried a map of the Northwest as then existed," Hugh Crawford is characterized as "an impressive figure, clad head to foot in buckskins, a large knife at his hip and his musket always in hand. The Indian guides would have no trouble from the hired hands while Hugh Crawford was around. His easy manner and pleasant demeanor immediately endeared him to the younger Englishmen he had come to lead" (Danson 173).

8. Estok defines ecophobia in "Theorizing in a Space of Ambivalent Openness."

9. Having received what he considered meager sums from the Board of Longitude and failed to get a fellowship from the Royal Society, Mason is described at the end of his life as being "embittered," "resentful," and "disillusioned" (Danson 201). But Pynchon depicts his condition as one of awakening, as Mason has at this stage shed much of his imperialist naiveté.

10. Discussions of nostalgia and history in *Underworld* can be found in Mraović-O'Hare and Staes.

11. The metaphor is refined in Gough 249–53.

12. On May 22, 1957, it was reported, an "Air Force B-36 bomber was ferrying a Mk 17 bomb weighing 42,000 lbs. (19,050 kg) from Biggs Air Force Base in Texas to Kirtland Air Force Base in New Mexico. During the landing approach, the bomb broke loose and tore part of the bomb bay doors off the plane as it fell. Although a retarding parachute deployed, it had little effect because of the plane's low altitude. The bomb's conventional explosives detonated as it impacted a cow pasture in Albuquerque just south of the base. The blast completely destroyed the bomb leaving a large crater 12 ft. (3.6 m) deep and 25 ft. (7.6 m) across. Debris was scattered over a wide area with some pieces found nearly a mile away. The weapon's nuclear capsule was aboard the plane but was carried separately eliminating the possibility of a nuclear detonation. Low levels of radioactivity were detected but were contained completely within the impact crater" ("Broken Arrow"). See also Maggelet and Oskins.

13. This refuge bears a resemblance to the proposed Jamie Whitten Wilderness Area in southeast Mississippi. In 1964 the US Atomic Energy Com-

mission detonated a nuclear bomb in the Tatum Salt Dome near Hattiesburg, Mississippi, to better "detect and calculate yields of similar underground tests that might be performed by the USSR" ("Salmon and Sterling"). The Atomic Energy Commission abandoned the site in 1972, and detonations performed at the Tatum Salt Dome were known, aptly, as "Project Dribble." The Department of Energy concedes leakage of low-level radioactive contamination in its 1996 Baseline Environmental Management Report.

14. The Watts Towers Arts Center website describes the installation as "consisting of seventeen major sculptures [. . .] created by Italian immigrant Sabato 'Simon' Rodia out of steel covered with mortar and embellished by the decorative finishings of mosaic tiles, glass, clay, shells and rock" ("Watts Towers").

15. The "Fresh Kills Park Project" page on the New York City Department of City Planning website describes plans for the landfill's future as a multiuse park, and the City of New York Parks and Recreation's "Freshkills Park" site describes its strategy to transform "the world's largest landfill into a productive and beautiful cultural destination" and "make the park a symbol of renewal and an expression of how our society can restore balance to its landscape" ("Freshkills Park").

16. From the *Bulletin of the Atomic Scientists*: "During the rainy, windy early morning of August 29, 1949, the Soviet Union conducted its first nuclear explosion—code-named 'First Lightning'—at the Semipalatinsk Test Site in eastern Kazakhstan. Witnesses remember feeling the ground tremble and seeing the sky turn red—and how that red sky was quickly dominated by a peculiar mushroom-shaped cloud. The Soviet military and scientific personnel conducting the test knew that the rain and wind would make the population more susceptible to radioactive fallout. But at the time, authorities disregarded the consequences for the sake of military and political goals. Throughout the next 40 years, such a trade-off would become all too familiar to those living at and around the test site. In all, the Soviet Union conducted 456 nuclear tests at Semipalatinsk (340 underground and 116 aboveground), starting with that first one in August 1949 and ending with the final test on October 19, 1989" ("Lasting Toll").

17. See West 102–3.

18. Relevant to this discussion are Hendin and chapter 6 of Giaimo. See also Tanner, "Afterthoughts" 63–71, and Gauthier 283–94.

19. Related approaches can be found in Sharp's *Savage Perils*. See also Blouin, Shipley, and Taylor.

Chapter 3

1. Ellison maintains that in order to quell protest in the "Southern Negro," the "North did four things: it promoted Negro education in the South; it controlled his economic and political destiny, or allowed the South to do so; it built Booker T. Washington into a national spokesman of Negroes with Tuskegee Institute as his seat of power; and it organized social science as an instrumentality to sanction its methods" (Ellison, *Collected Essays* 330). Warren reports that Ellison "decries" Washington's "Tuskegee Machine," because in his

opinion the college served "to deflect Negro energy from direct political action" (qtd. in Warren 32).

2. The European Starling, an invasive species in the United States, was released in 1890 as "part of a plan to introduce to the U.S. all birds mentioned in the works of Shakespeare" ("European Starling").

3. Symbolic birds and other folk influences on Ellison's work are documented in Blake.

4. Abjection of this kind can also be found in the tumultuous Golden Day, a bar and house of ill repute where the Invisible Man takes Norton after Trueblood's performance. Scholars have noted that the name "Golden Day" is derived from Lewis Mumford's book *The Golden Day: A Study in American Experience and Culture* (1926). Chapter 4 of Nadel's *Invisible Criticism* explains that at the Golden Day, readers are "beginning to see two worlds, one of white trustees and schools, and one of bars, bordellos, and tenant farmers. The invisible man's charge is to keep the two separate. The school, in other words, wants to present a façade of black life" (95).

5. Ellison explains during his lecture "Education for Culturally Different Youth" that the "things which come at you in a Negro grade school are just as diverse as those which will come at you in an upper-class white school. The question is how you can relate the environment to yourself? How can one discover, for instance, that well-cooked chitterlings are part of a cuisine? It took me a lot of living and going to France to realize this obvious fact. I said to myself, 'what on earth are these Frenchmen doing? This is peasant food—chitterlings are peasant food. There are some great masters of Negro cooking. Chitterlings must be a part of a high low-class cuisine!'" (Ellison, *Going* 67).

6. Just after meeting Brother Jack, the Invisible Man returns to Mary's apartment and hears her singing "Back Water Blues," a song about dispossession, flooding, and environmental change recorded by Bessie Smith in 1927 and by Lead Belly in 1944: "When it thunders and lightning, and the wind begins to blow / There's thousands of people ain't got no place to go" (Springer 25).

7. As Singer explains, any "mention of science or machinery always signals danger in *Invisible Man*" (393).

8. See Roos 229–50.

9. Gikandi explains that "if we perceive exile as something akin to the liminal phase in the ritual process, Caribbean writers write about, and within, an indeterminate space between the colonial economy of representation and the desired national culture" (41). "Limbo," Prior argues, "is a borderland. It is neither heaven nor hell, and whoever resides there is in a space where the perspective used to see into other worlds will not be governed by those worlds' norms. If one accepts that novels such as *Palace of the Peacock*, or poems such as *Omeros* and *Turner*, have settings that are outside the literary norms of sequential narrative and fixed or 'solid' settings and characters, then limbo, with all the further connotations that may be applied, becomes both an explanatory and an enriching term" (588).

10. Ramazani examines Philoctete's scar in "Wound of History." Also see Fumagalli and Patrick.

11. See Ramazani, *Hybrid*.

12. For an alternate representation of Helen, see "Menelaus" in *The Arkansas Testament.* Approaching Ma Kilman as in "island body" problematizes Burnett's argument that "Walcott develops the traditional association of the land with the female body, sensualizing St. Lucia by pairing it with its female protagonist Helen, a move which might be regarded as repeating a long-established sexist stereotype if it were not for the way he uses his strategy. He takes the myth of the island as Helen—a given provided by St. Lucian History—in order to detach it from its Eurocentric roots and naturalize it to his own society" (294). Jay also dissects the poem's "romantic idealization of Helen" and makes the point that she "cannot stand as a metaphor for the island because the island must be seen without the light of metaphor, beyond the 'Homeric shadow'" (550). Other critical works that explore the figure of Helen include Figueroa, Lock, McClure, and Minkler.

13. See Austenfeld.

14. More on the *paille-banane* dance can be found in Carchidi 219.

15. In "Isla Incognita," Walcott expresses this sentiment in another way: "It has taken me over thirty years, and my race hundreds, to feel the fibers spread from the splayed toes and grip this earth, the arms knot into boles and put out leaves. When that begins, this is the beginning of season, cycle time. The noise my leaves make is my language. In it is tunneled the roar of seas of a lost ocean. It is a fresh sound" (57).

16. In response to the construction of the Hilton Jalousie Hotel in an ecologically sensitive volcanic region near Soufriére, Walcott worries that the people of St. Lucia have "settled down into an idea that tourism is the alternative to agriculture." He adds, "I don't like the dependency of thinking that the generosity of tourism becomes the equivalent of a waiter looking for a big tip, and depending on that big tip for sustenance, for his livelihood" (Walcott, "Argument" 127).

Chapter 4

1. A concise treatment of Romero's *Night of the Living Dead* can be found in chapter 3 of Bishop's *American Zombie Gothic* (2010). See also Tony Williams's *The Cinema of George A. Romero* (2003) and Gagne's *The Zombies That Ate Pittsburgh* (1987).

2. In "A Zombie Manifesto," Lauro and Embry argue that the "zombie horde is a swarm" (89) and wonder "which is more terrifying: our ultimate separation from our fellow humans, or the dystopic fantasy of a swarm organism" (101).

3. Post-9/11 zombie movies of note include *28 Days Later* (2002), *Resident Evil* (2002), and the remake of *Dawn of the Dead* (2004). See also dark satires *Shaun of the Dead* (2004) and *Fido* (2006). Books include Brooks's *The Zombie Survival Guide* (2003) and *World War Z* (2006), Keene's *The Rising* (2004), and Ralph's graphic novel *Daybreak* (2011).

4. See Moreman and Rushton's *Race, Oppression and the Zombie.* Murphy's "White Zombie" and Carpio's "Conjuring the Mysteries of Slavery" also contextualize zombie lore for a contemporary audience.

5. A collection of early zombie comics that illustrates this transition can be found in Wood, Yoe, Banes, and Gussoni's *Zombies* (2002).

6. Delfino and Taylor's "Walking Contradictions" is a most tasteful study of zombie physiology.

7. McCloud offers a convincing rationale for why comics warrant closer scholarly scrutiny. Also helpful are Gardner, Lefèvre, and Chaney.

8. Characterizing *Oryx and Crake* as a dystopian bookend and sequel to *The Handmaid's Tale* (1985) denies this book much of its ecocritical currency; as a novel of liminal topographies, I think *Oryx and Crake* fits better as a sequel and companion piece to Atwood's novel *Surfacing* (1972). Both *Surfacing* and *Oryx and Crake* highlight literary figures with problems of self-classification as they observe at-risk natural environments. Both novels explore the correlation between imperiled landscapes and transitional human identities, and their central figures lose their names, with reclamation intimately linked to their changing relationships to the natural world. As mentioned, the "Historical Notes" at the end of *The Handmaid's Tale* does reveal an optimism similar to *1984* and, in one important sense, *Oryx and Crake.*

9. "Biodiversity will increase . . . as buildings tumble and smash into each other," Alan Weisman suggests in *The World Without Us* (2007), "and lime from crushed concrete raises soil pH, inviting in trees" (33).

10. Actual scientific "splices" such as "luminous green rabbits" (*OC* 96) and the spoat/gider" (199) are described alongside mood-enhancing wallpaper with a "modified form of Kirilian energy-sensing algae embedded in it" (201) and walls "made of a new mussle-adhesive/silicon/dendrite-formation alloy, ultra-resistant" (297).

11. For an analysis of power dynamics in *The Year of the Flood,* see Sheckels 153–62.

12. See also Vint's *Animal Alterity* for an in-depth discussion of science-fiction representations of animal life.

13. From an ecocritical standpoint, the term "eugenic environmentalism" might have more efficacy in a study of the Crakers, a humanoid species with marked morphological, behavioral, sexual, and intellectual differences from the *Homo sapiens* with whom they interact and ultimately mate. Larger nuclear families with many children, which historically correlate with patriarchal structures and reduced access to birth control, won't hold water as a harbinger for liberation politics in Atwood's trilogy, as "reproductive rights" for women in the Western Hemisphere has rarely meant the right to have more children.

14. For a primer on the current honey bee crisis, see Jacobsen.

Works Cited

1996 Baseline Environmental Management Report, The. Washington: U.S. Dept. of Energy, Office of Environmental Management, Office of Strategic Planning and Analysis, 1996. Print.

Adams, Clementina R. "The Endless Rains of Death and Desolation in García Márquez's Short Stories." *Climate and Literature: Reflections on the Environment.* Ed. Janet Pérez and Wendell Aycock. Lubbock: Texas Tech UP, 1995. 65-72. Print.

Adams, Rachel. "The Ends of America, the Ends of Postmodernism." *Twentieth-Century Literature* 53.3 (2007): 248-72. Print.

Allaire, Franklin. "The Only Good Walker Is a Dead Walker." *The Walking Dead and Philosophy.* Ed. Wayne Yuen. Chicago: Open Court, 2012. 195-206. Print.

Anderson, Christopher Todd. "Sacred Waste: Ecology, Spirit, and the American Garbage Poem." *ISLE* 17.1 (2010): 35-60. Print.

Armbruster, Karla, and Kathleen R. Wallace. "Introduction: Why Go Beyond Nature Writing, and Where To?" *Beyond Nature Writing: Expanding the Boundaries of Ecocriticism.* Ed. Karla Armbruster and Kathleen R. Wallace. Charlottesville: UP of Virginia, 2001. 1-25. Print.

Atwood, Margaret. *The Handmaid's Tale.* New York: Anchor Books, 1998. Print.

——. "*The Handmaid's Tale* and *Oryx and Crake* in Context." *PMLA* 119.3 (2004): 513-17. Print.

——. *MaddAddam.* New York: Doubleday, 2013. Print.

——. *Oryx and Crake.* New York: Anchor Books, 2004. Print.

——. *Surfacing.* New York: Anchor Books, 1998. Print.

——. *The Year of the Flood.* New York: Random House, 2009. Print.

Atwood, Margaret, and Earl G. Ingersoll. *Margaret Atwood: Conversations.* Princeton: Ontario Review Press, 1990. Print.

Austenfeld, Thomas. "How to Begin a New World: Dante in Walcott's *Omeros.*" *South Atlantic Review* 71.3 (2006): 15-28. Print.

Baker, Houston A., Jr. *Blues, Ideology, and Afro-American Culture.* Chicago: U of Chicago P, 1984. Print.

Barnacle, Hugo. "The End Is Nigh." Rev. of *Oryx and Crake, by Margaret Atwood. New Statesman* 19 May 2003: 50. Web. 4 June 2009. <http://www.newstatesman.com/node/145492>.

Barnhill, David Landis. "Critical Utopianism and Bioregional Ecocriticism."

The Bioregional Imagination: Literature, Ecology, and Place. Ed. Tom Lynch, Cheryll Glotfelty, and Karla Armbruster. Athens: U of Georgia P, 2012. 212–25. Print.

Bell-Villada, Gene H. "Banana Strike and Military Massacre: *One Hundred Years of Solitude* and What Happened in 1928." *Gabriel García Márquez's* One Hundred Years of Solitude*: A Casebook.* Ed. Gene H. Bell-Villada. Oxford: Oxford UP, 2002. 127–38. Print.

——. *García Márquez: The Man and His Work.* Chapel Hill: U of North Carolina P, 2010. Print.

Benítez-Rojo, Antonio. *The Repeating Island: The Caribbean and the Postmodern Perspective.* Durham: Duke UP, 1992. Print.

Bergthaller, Hannes. "Housebreaking the Human Animal: Humanism and the Problem of Sustainability in Margaret Atwood's *Oryx and Crake* and *The Year of the Flood.*" *English Studies* 91.7 (2010): 728–43. Print.

Bhabha, Homi K. *The Location of Culture.* New York: Routledge, 2004. Print.

Bishop, Kyle W. *American Zombie Gothic: The Rise and Fall (and Rise) of the Walking Dead in Popular Culture.* Jefferson: McFarland, 2010. Print.

——. "The Idle Proletariat: *Dawn of the Dead,* Consumer Ideology, and the Loss of Productive Labor." *Journal of Popular Culture* 43.2 (2010): 234–48. Print.

Blake, Susan L. "Ritual and Rationalization: Black Folklore in the Works of Ralph Ellison." *Ralph Ellison.* Ed. Harold Bloom. New York: Chelsea House, 1986. 77–99. Print.

Blouin, Michael, Morgan Shipley, and Jack Taylor. *The Silence of Fallout: Nuclear Criticism in a Post-Cold War World.* Newcastle on Tyne, UK: Cambridge Scholars, 2013. Print.

Boon, Kevin. "The Zombie as Other: Mortality and the Monstrous in the Post-Nuclear Age." *Better Off Dead: The Evolution of the Zombie as Post-Human.* Ed. Deborah Christie and Sarah Juliet Lauro. New York: Fordham UP, 2011. 50–60. Print.

Bouson, J. Brooks. "'It's Game Over Forever': Atwood's Satiric Vision of a Bioengineered Posthuman Future in *Oryx and Crake.*" *Journal of Commonwealth Literature* 39.3 (2004): 139–56. Print.

Boxall, Peter. *Don DeLillo: The Possibility of Fiction.* New York: Routledge, 2006.

Boyagoda, Anna. "'Why Should He Be Here, Why Should They Have Come at All?': Transnational Community in Derek Walcott's *Omeros.*" *Atenea* 27.1 (2007): 79–92. Print.

Braziel, Jana Evans. "'Caribbean Genesis': Language, Gardens, Worlds (Jamaica Kincaid, Derek Walcott, Édouard Glissant)." *Caribbean Literature and the Environment: Between Nature and Culture.* Ed. Elizabeth M. DeLoughrey, Renée K. Gosson, and George B. Handley. Charlottesville: UP of Virginia, 2005. 110–26. Print.

"Broken Arrow Nuclear Weapons Accidents." *Aerospaceweb.org.* 2 April 2006. Web. 14 May 2013. <http://www.aerospaceweb.org/question/weapons/q0268.shtml>.

Brooker, Will. "The Blade Runner Experience: Pilgrimage and Liminal Space." *The Blade Runner Experience: The Legacy of a Science Fiction Classic.* Ed. Will Brooker. London: Wallflower, 2005. 11–30. Print.

Brooks, Max. *World War Z: An Oral History of the Zombie War.* New York: Crown, 2006. Print.

Brooks, Max, and Max Werner. *The Zombie Survival Guide: Complete Protection from the Living Dead.* London: Duckworth, 2004. Print.

Bryson, Michael A. *Visions of the Land: Science, Literature, and the American Environment from the Era of Exploration to the Age of Ecology.* Charlottesville: UP of Virginia, 2002. Print.

Buell, Lawrence. *The Future of Environmental Criticism: Environmental Crisis and Literary Imagination.* Malden: Blackwell, 2005. Print.

——. *Writing for an Endangered World: Literature, Culture, and Environment in the U.S. and Beyond.* Cambridge: Harvard UP, 2001. Print.

Burian, Peter. "'All That Greek Manure under the Green Bananas': Derek Walcott's Odyssey." *South Atlantic Quarterly* 96.2 (1997): 359–77. Print.

Burnett, Paula. "The Island Self as World Text in the Work of Derek Walcott and Romesh Gunesekera." *Routes of the Roots: Geography and Literature in the English-Speaking Countries.* Ed. Isabella M. Zoppi. Rome: Bulzoni, 1998. 289–307. Print.

Callahan, Lance. *In the Shadows of Divine Perfection: Derek Walcott's* Omeros. New York: Routledge, 2003. Print.

Carchidi, Victoria. "'Heaven Is a Green Place': Varieties of Spiritual Landscape in Caribbean Literature." *Mapping the Sacred: Religion, Geography and Postcolonial Literatures.* Ed. Jamie S. Scott and Paul Simpson-Housley. Amsterdam: Rodopi, 2001. Print.

Carpio, Glenda R. "Conjuring the Mysteries of Slavery: Voodoo, Fetishism, and Stereotype in Ishmael Reed's 'Flight to Canada.'" *American Literature* 77.3 (2005): 563–89. Print.

Casid, Jill H. "Chimerical Figurations at the Monstrous Edges of Species." *Environmental Criticism for the Twenty-First Century.* Ed. Stephanie LeMenager, Teresa Shewry, and Ken Hiltner. New York: Routledge, 2011. 61–83. Print.

Cavalieri, Nate, Adam Skolnick, and Wendy Yanagihara. *Costa Rica.* Footscray: Lonely Planet, 2012. Print.

Chaney, Michael A. "Animal Subjects of the Graphic Novel." *College Literature* 38.3 (2011): 129–49. Print.

Christie, Deborah. "A Dead New World: Richard Matheson and the Modern Zombie." *Better Off Dead: The Evolution of the Zombie as Post-Human.* Ed. Deborah Christie and Sarah Juliet Lauro. New York: Fordham UP, 2011. 67–80. Print.

Chuh, Kandice. "Of Hemispheres and Other Spheres: Navigating Karen Tei Yamashita's Literary World." *American Literary History* 18.3 (2006): 618–37. Print.

Cohen, Samuel. "*Mason & Dixon* & the Ampersand." *Twentieth-Century Literature* 48.3 (2002): 264–91. Print.

Collado-Rodriguez, Francisco. "*Mason & Dixon,* Historiographic Metafiction, and the Unstable Reconciliation of Opposites." *American Postmodernity: Essays on the Recent Fiction of Thomas Pynchon.* Ed. Ian D. Copestake. New York: Peter Lang, 2003. 71–81. Print.

Conniff, Brian. "The Dark Side of Magical Realism: Science, Oppression, and Apocalypse in *One Hundred Years of Solitude.*" *Gabriel García Márquez's* One

Hundred Years of Solitude*: A Casebook.* Ed. Gene H. Bell-Villada. Oxford: Oxford UP, 2002. 139–52. Print.

Cornis-Pope, Marcel. *Narrative Innovation and Cultural Rewriting in the Cold War and After.* New York: Palgrave, 2001. Print.

Cowart, David. "The Luddite Vision: *Mason & Dixon.*" *American Literature* 71.2 (1999): 341–63. Print.

Danson, Edwin. *Drawing the Line: How Mason and Dixon Surveyed the Most Famous Border in America.* New York: John Wiley, 2001. Print.

Dash, J. M. *The Other America: Caribbean Literature in a New World Context.* Charlottesville: UP of Virginia, 1998. Print.

Davis, H. Louise. "Natural Resistance: Margaret Atwood as Ecofeminist or Apocalyptic Visionary." *Women Writing Nature: A Feminist View.* Ed. Barbara J. Cook. Lanham: Lexington Books, 2008. 81–94. Print.

Delfino, Robert A., and Kyle Taylor. "Walking Contradictions." *The Walking Dead and Philosophy.* Ed. Wayne Yuen. Chicago: Open Court, 2012. 39–51. Print.

DeLillo, Don. *Underworld.* New York: Scribner, 1997. Print.

Dewey, Joseph. "The Sound of One Man Mapping: Wicks Cherrycoke and the Eastern (Re)solution." *Pynchon and* Mason & Dixon. Ed. Brooke Horvath and Irving Malin. Newark: U of Delaware P, 2000. 112–31. Print.

Dillon, Grace L. "Introduction." *Walking the Clouds: An Anthology of Indigenous Science Fiction.* Ed. Grace L. Dillon. Tucson: U of Arizona P, 2012. 1-12. Print.

DiMarco, Danette. "Paradice Lost, Paradise Regained: *Homo Faber* and the Makings of a New Beginning in *Oryx and Crake.*" *Papers on Language and Literature* 41.2 (2005): 170–95. Print.

Dixon, Melvin. *Ride Out the Wilderness: Geography and Identity in Afro-American Literature.* Urbana: U of Illinois P, 1987. Print.

Dunning, Stephen. "Margaret Atwood's *Oryx and Crake*: The Terror of the Therapeutic." *Canadian Literature* 186 (2005): 86–101. Print.

Elbow, Gary S. "Creating an Atmosphere: Depiction of Climate in the Works of Gabriel García Márquez." *Climate and Literature: Reflections on the Environment.* Ed. Janet Pérez and Wendell Aycock. Lubbock: Texas Tech UP, 1995. 73–81. Print.

Eliot, T. S. *The Waste Land and Other Writings.* New York: Modern Library, 2002. 38–58. Print.

Ellison, Ralph. *The Collected Essays of Ralph Ellison.* New York: Modern Library, 1995. Print.

——. *Going to the Territory.* New York: Random House, 1986. Print.

——. *Invisible Man.* 1952. New York: Vintage, 1995. Print.

Ellison, Ralph, and Albert Murray. *Trading Twelves: The Selected Letters of Ralph Ellison and Albert Murray.* New York: Modern Library, 2000. Print.

Estok, Simon C. "Theorizing in a Space of Ambivalent Openness: Ecocriticism and Ecophobia." *ISLE* 16.2 (2009): 203–25. Print.

"European Starling." *National Invasive Species Information Center.* USDA. 20 June 2012. Web. 26 September 2012. <http://www.invasivespeciesinfo.gov/animals/eurostarling.shtml>.

Evans, David H. "Taking Out the Trash: Don DeLillo's *Underworld,* Liquid Modernity, and the End of Garbage." *Cambridge Quarterly* 35:2 (2006): 103–32. Print.

Evernden, Neil. "Beyond Ecology: Self, Place, and the Pathetic Fallacy." *The Ecocriticism Reader: Landmarks in Literary Ecology.* Ed. Cheryll Glotfelty and Harold Fromm. Athens: U of Georgia P, 1996. 92–104. Print.

Farrell, Joseph. "Walcott's *Omeros*: The Classical Epic in a Postmodern World." *South Atlantic Quarterly* 96.2 (1997): 247–73. Print.

"feng-shui, n." *OED Web.* September 2012. Oxford U. Web. 19 November 2012. <http://www.oed.com>.

Figueroa, Víctor. "Encomium of Helen: Derek Walcott's Ethical Twist in *Omeros*." *Twentieth-Century Literature* 53.1 (2007): 23–39. Print.

"Freshkills Park." *NYC Parks.* 2015. Web. 12 December 2015. <http://www.nycgovparks.org/park-features/freshkills-park/about-the-site >.

"Fresh Kills Park Project." *NYCPlanning.* 2013. Web. 14 May 2013. <http://www.nyc.gov/html/dcp/html/fkl/fkl_index.shtml>.

Fumagalli, Maria C., and Peter L. Patrick. "Two Healing Narratives: Suffering, Reintegration, and the Struggle of Language." *Small Axe: A Caribbean Journal of Criticism* 10.2 (2006): 61–79. Print.

Gagne, Paul R. *The Zombies That Ate Pittsburgh: The Films of George A. Romero.* New York: Dodd, Mead, 1987. Print.

Gamber, John B. *Positive Pollutions and Cultural Toxins: Waste and Contamination in Contemporary U.S. Ethnic Literatures.* Lincoln: U of Nebraska P, 2012. Print.

García Márquez, Gabriel. *Love in the Time of Cholera.* New York: Knopf, 1988. Print.

——. "Nobel Lecture: The Solitude of Latin America." *Nobelprize.org.* Nobel Media. 2013. Web. 28 Jul 2013. <http://www.nobelprize.org/nobel_prizes/literature/laureates/1982/marquez-lecture.html >.

——. *One Hundred Years of Solitude.* 1967. New York: Harper Perennial, 2006. Print.

Gardner, Jared. *Projections: Comics and the History of Twenty-First-Century Storytelling.* Stanford: Stanford UP, 2012. Print.

Garrard, Greg. *Ecocriticism.* New York: Routledge, 2004. Print.

Gauthier, Marni. "Better Living through Westward Migration: Don DeLillo's Inversion of the American West as 'Virgin Land' in *Underworld*." *Moving Stories: Migration and the American West, 1850–2000.* Ed. Scott E. Casper and Lucinda M. Long. Reno: Nevada Humanities Committee, 2001. 275–96. Print.

Gennep, Arnold van. *The Rites of Passage.* 1908. Chicago: U of Chicago P, 1960. Print.

Giaimo, Paul. *Appreciating Don DeLillo: The Moral Force of a Writer's Work.* Santa Barbara: Praeger, 2011. Print.

Gikandi, Simon. *Writing in Limbo: Modernism and Caribbean Culture.* Ithaca: Cornell UP, 1992. Print.

Gleason, Paul. "Don DeLillo, T. S. Eliot, and the Redemption of America's Atomic Waste Land." *UnderWords: Perspectives on Don DeLillo's* Underworld. Ed. Joseph Dewey, Steven G. Kellman, and Irving Malin. Newark: U of Delaware P, 2002. 130–43. Print.

Glissant, Édouard, and J. M. Dash. *Caribbean Discourse: Selected Essays.* Charlottesville: UP of Virginia, 1992. Print.

Gonzales, Sarah. "Grave New World." Rev. of *Oryx and Crake,* by Margaret Atwood. Ms. 13.2 (2003): 91. Print.

Gough, Annette. "Body/Mine: A Chaos Narrative of Cyborg Subjectivities and Liminal Experiences." *Women's Studies: An Interdisciplinary Journal* 34.3-4 (2005): 249-64. Print.

"Great Serpent Mound." Heilbrunn Timeline of Art History. *The Metropolitan Museum of Art.* October 2002. Web. 19 November 2012. <http://www.metmuseum.org/toah/hd/serp/hd_serp.htm>.

Hamner, Robert D. *Epic of the Dispossessed: Derek Walcott's* Omeros. Columbia: U of Missouri P, 1997.

Hanford, Robin. "The Land and the Language: Derek Walcott and St. Lucia." *Routes of the Roots: Geography and Literature in the English-Speaking Countries.* Ed. Isabella M. Zoppi. Rome: Bulzoni, 1998. 751-67. Print.

Hanson, David, Edwin Marty, and Michael Hanson. *Breaking through Concrete: Building an Urban Farm Revival.* Berkeley: U of California P, 2012. Print.

Hardack, Richard. "World Trade Centers and World-Wide-Webs: From *Underworld* to Over-Soul in Don DeLillo." *Arizona Quarterly* 69.1 (2013): 151-83. Print.

Harris, Michael. "Pynchon's Postcoloniality." *Thomas Pynchon: Reading from the Margins.* Ed. Niran Abbas. Madison: Fairleigh Dickinson UP, 2003. 199-214. Print.

Hatch, Ronald B. "Margaret Atwood, the Land, and Ecology." *Margaret Atwood: Works and Impact.* Ed. Reingard M. Nischik. Rochester: Camden House, 2000. 180-201. Print.

Heise, Ursula K. "Ecocriticism and the Transnational Turn in American Studies." *American Literary History* 20.1 (2008): 381-404. Print.

——. "Local Rock and Global Plastic: World Ecology and the Experience of Place." *Comparative Literature Studies* 41.1 (2004): 126-52. Print.

Helyer, Ruth. "'Refuse Heaped Many Stories High': DeLillo, Dirt, and Disorder." *Modern Fiction Studies* 45.4 (1999): 987-1006. Print.

Henderson, Mae. *Borders, Boundaries, and Frames: Essays in Cultural Criticism and Cultural Studies.* New York: Routledge, 1995. Print.

Hendin, Josephine Gattuso. "*Underworld,* Ethnicity, and Found Object Art: Reason and Revelation." *Don DeLillo:* Mao II, Underworld, Falling Man. Ed. Stacey Olster. London: Continuum, 2011. 99-115. Print.

Hengen, Shannon. "Margaret Atwood and Environmentalism." *The Cambridge Companion to Margaret Atwood.* Ed. Coral Ann Howells. Cambridge: Cambridge UP, 2006. 72-85. Print.

Higonnet, Margaret R. *Borderwork: Feminist Engagements with Comparative Literature.* Ithaca: Cornell UP, 1994. Print.

Hill, Michael D., and Lena M. Hill. *Ralph Ellison's Invisible Man: A Reference Guide.* Westport: Greenwood Press, 2008. Print.

Hinds, Elizabeth Jane Wall. "Animal, Vegetable, Mineral: The Play of Species in Pynchon's *Mason & Dixon.*" *Human and Other Animals in Eighteenth-Century Culture: Representation, Hybridity, Ethics.* Ed. Frank Palmeri. Burlington: Ashgate, 2006. 179-99. Print.

———. "Introduction: The Times of *Mason & Dixon*." *The Multiple Worlds of Pynchon's* Mason & Dixon: *Eighteenth-Century Contexts, Postmodern Observations*. Ed. Elizabeth Jane Wall Hinds. Rochester: Camden House, 2005. 3-24. Print.

Hird, Myra J. *The Origins of Sociable Life: Evolution after Science Studies*. New York: Palgrave Macmillan, 2009. Print.

Holy Bible. King James Version. New York: Books, Inc., 1962. Print.

Honey, Martha. *Ecotourism and Sustainable Development: Who Owns Paradise?* Washington: Island Press, 2008. Print.

Howells, Coral Ann. "Bad News." Rev. of *Oryx and Crake*, by Margaret Atwood. *Canadian Literature* 183 (2004): 92–93. Print.

———. "Margaret Atwood's Dystopian Visions: *The Handmaid's Tale* and *Oryx and Crake*." *The Cambridge Companion to Margaret Atwood*. Ed. Coral Ann Howells. Cambridge: Cambridge UP, 2006. 161–75. Print.

———. "*Oryx and Crake*." *Margaret Atwood*. New York: Palgrave Macmillan, 2005. 170–84. Print.

Howse, Derek. *Nevil Maskelyne, the Seaman's Astronomer*. Cambridge: Cambridge UP, 1989. Print.

Huggan, Graham, and Helen Tiffin. *Postcolonial Ecocriticism: Literature, Animals, Environment*. New York: Routledge, 2010. Print.

Humes, Edward. *Garbology: Our Dirty Love Affair with Trash*. New York: Avery, 2012. Print.

Ingersoll, Earl G. "Survival in Margaret Atwood's Novel *Oryx and Crake*." *Extrapolation* 45.2 (2004): 162–75. Print.

Inness, Sherrie A., and Diana Royer. *Breaking Boundaries: New Perspectives on Women's Regional Writing*. Iowa City: U of Iowa P, 1997. Print.

Isaacson, Johanna. "Postmodern Wastelands: *Underworld* and the Productive Failures of Periodization." *Criticism* 54.1 (2012): 29–58. Print.

Jacobsen, Rowan. *Fruitless Fall: The Collapse of the Honey Bee and the Coming Agricultural Crisis*. New York: Bloomsbury, 2009. Print.

Janes, Regina. *Gabriel García Márquez: Revolutions in Wonderland*. Columbia: U of Missouri P, 1981. Print.

———. "Revisiting García Márquez among the Bananas." *Modern Language Quarterly* 71.4 (2010): 453–77. Print.

Jarenski, Shelly. "Invisibility Embraced: The Abject as a Site of Agency in Ellison's *Invisible Man*." *MELUS* 35.4 (2010): 85-109. Print.

Jay, Paul. "Fated to Unoriginality: The Politics of Mimicry in Derek Walcott's *Omeros*." *Callaloo* 29.2 (2006): 545–59. Print.

Kaplan, Gisela T., and Lesley J. Rogers. *Gene Worship: Moving beyond the Nature/Nurture Debate over Genes, Brain, and Gender*. New York: Other Press, 2003. Print.

Kaplan, Rachel, and K. Ruby Blume. *Urban Homesteading: Heirloom Skills for Sustainable Living*. New York: Skyhorse, 2011. Print.

Keck, Charles. *Lifting the Veil of Ignorance*. 1922. Sculpture. Tuskegee University, Tuskegee, Alabama.

Keene, Brian. *The Rising*. New York: Leisure Books/Dorchester, 2003. Print.

Keller, David R. "Toward a Post-Mechanistic Philosophy of Nature." *ISLE* 16.4 (2009): 709–25. Print.

Kennedy, William. *Riding the Yellow Trolley Car: Selected Nonfiction.* New York: Viking, 1993. Print.

Kirkman, Robert, Charles Adlard, Tony Moore, and Cliff Rathburn. *The Walking Dead Compendium One.* Berkeley: Image Comics, 2009. Print.

Klein, Philip S., and Ari Hoogenboom. *A History of Pennsylvania.* New York: McGraw-Hill, 1973. Print.

Krasteva, Yonka. "Chaos and Pattern in Ellison's *Invisible Man.*" *Southern Literary Journal* 30.1 (1997): 55–72. Print.

"Lasting Toll of Semipalatinsk's Nuclear Testing, The." *Bulletin of the Atomic Scientists.* 28 September 2009. Web. 14 May 2013. <http://thebulletin.org/lasting-toll-semipalatinsks-nuclear-testing>.

Lauro, Sarah J., and Karen Embry. "A Zombie Manifesto: The Nonhuman Condition in the Era of Advanced Capitalism." *Boundary 2* 35.1 (2008): 85–108. Print.

Lavender III, Isiah. "Introduction." *Black and Brown Planets: The Politics of Race in Science Fiction.* Ed. Isiah Lavender III. Jackson: UP of Mississippi, 2014. 3–11. Print.

Lee, Sue-Im. "'We Are Not the World': Global Village, Universalism, and Karen Tei Yamashita's *Tropic of Orange.*" *Modern Fiction Studies* 53.3 (2007): 501–27. Print.

Lefèvre, Pascal. "The Construction of Space in Comics." *A Comics Studies Reader.* Ed. Jeet Heer and Kent Worcester. Jackson: UP of Mississippi, 2009. 157–62. Print.

Legler, Gretchen T. "Ecofeminist Literary Criticism." *Ecofeminism: Women, Culture, Nature.* Ed. Karen J. Warren. Bloomington: Indiana UP, 1997. 227–38. Print.

Leland, John. *Aliens in the Backyard: Plant and Animal Imports into America.* Columbia: U of South Carolina P, 2005. Print.

LeMenager, Stephanie, Teresa Shewry, and Ken Hiltner. "Introduction." *Environmental Criticism for the Twenty-First Century.* Ed. Stephanie LeMenager, Teresa Shewry, and Ken Hiltner. New York: Routledge, 2011. 1–15. Print.

Lensing, Dennis M. "Postmodernism at Sea: The Quest for Longitude in Thomas Pynchon's *Mason & Dixon* and Umberto Eco's *The Island of the Day Before.*" *The Multiple Worlds of Pynchon's* Mason & Dixon: *Eighteenth-Century Contexts, Postmodern Observations.* Ed. Elizabeth Jane Wall Hinds. Rochester: Camden House, 2005. 125–43. Print.

Llarull, Gustavo. "The Long and Winding Road of Technology from *María* to *Cien años de soledad* to *Mantra*: An Ecocritical Reading." *The Natural World in Latin American Literatures: Ecocritical Essays on Twentieth Century Writings.* Ed. Adrian T. Kane. Jefferson: McFarland, 2010. 89–110. Print.

Lock, Charles. "Derek Walcott's *Omeros*: Echoes from a White-Throated Vase." *Massachusetts Review* 41.1 (2000): 9–31. Print.

"Luo Pan Chinese Compass, The." *Feng Shui Institute.* 7 August 2012. Web. 19 November 2012. < http://www.feng-shui-institute.org/luopan.htm>.

Lynch, Tom, Cheryll Glotfelty, and Karla Armbruster. "Introduction." *The Bioregional Imagination: Literature, Ecology, and Place.* Ed. Tom Lynch, Cheryll Glotfelty, and Karla Armbruster. Athens: U of Georgia P, 2012. 1–29. Print.

Maggelet, Michael H., and James C. Oskins. *Broken Arrow: The Declassified History of U.S. Nuclear Weapons Accidents.* Raleigh: Lulu.com, 2007. Print.

Margulis, Lynn. *Symbiotic Planet: A New Look at Evolution.* New York: Basic Books, 1998. Print.

Martin, Gerald. *Gabriel García Márquez: A Life.* New York: Knopf, 2009. Print.

Martucci, Elise A. *The Environmental Unconscious in the Fiction of Don DeLillo.* New York: Routledge, 2007. Print.

Marx, Leo. *The Machine in the Garden: Technology and the Pastoral Ideal in America.* 1964. Oxford: Oxford UP, 2000. Print.

Mason, Charles, and Jeremiah Dixon. *The Journal of Charles Mason and Jeremiah Dixon.* Philadelphia: American Philosophical Society, 1969. Print.

McCloud, Scott. *Understanding Comics: The Invisible Art.* New York: Harper Perennial, 1994. Print.

McClure, Charlotte S. "Helen of the 'West Indies': History or Poetry of a Caribbean Realm." *Studies in the Literary Imagination* 26.2 (1993): 7–20. Print.

McDonough, William, and Michael Braungart. *The Upcycle: Beyond Sustainability, Designing for Abundance.* New York: North Point Press, 2013. Print.

McGowan, Todd. "The Obsolescence of Mystery and the Accumulation of Waste in Don DeLillo's *Underworld.*" *Critique* 46.2 (2005): 123–45. Print.

McHale, Brian. "*Mason & Dixon* in the Zone, or, A Brief Poetics of Pynchon-Space." *Pynchon and* Mason & Dixon. Ed. Brooke Horvath and Irving Malin. Newark: U of Delaware P, 2000. 43–62. Print.

McLaughlin, Robert L. "Surveying, Mapmaking and Representation in *Mason & Dixon.*" *American Postmodernity: Essays on the Recent Fiction of Thomas Pynchon.* Ed. Ian D. Copestake. New York: Peter Lang, 2003. 173–91. Print.

McMurray, George R. "The Role of Climate Change in Twentieth-Century Spanish American Fiction." *Climate and Literature: Reflections on the Environment.* Ed. Janet Pérez and Wendell Aycock. Lubbock: Texas Tech UP, 1995. 55–64. Print.

Melas, Natalie. "Forgettable Vacations and Metaphor in Ruins: Walcott's *Omeros.*" *Callaloo* 28.1 (2005): 147–68. Print.

Mermann-Jozwiak, Elisabeth. "Yamashita's Post-National Spaces: 'It All Comes Together in Los Angeles.'" *Canadian Review of American Studies* 41.1 (2011): 1–24. Print.

Millard, William B. "Delineations of Madness and Science: *Mason & Dixon,* Pynchonian Space and the Snovian Disjunction." *American Postmodernity: Essays on the Recent Fiction of Thomas Pynchon.* Ed. Ian D. Copestake. New York: Peter Lang, 2003. 83–127. Print.

Minkler, Julie A. "Helen's Calibans: A Study of Gender Hierarchy in Derek Walcott's *Omeros.*" *World Literature Today* 67.2 (1993): 272–76. Print.

Moreman, Christopher M., and Cory Rushton. *Race, Oppression and the Zombie: Essays on Cross-Cultural Appropriations of the Caribbean Tradition.* Jefferson: McFarland, 2011. Print.

——. *Zombies Are Us: Essays on the Humanity of the Walking Dead.* Jefferson: McFarland, 2011. Print.

Morton, Timothy. *The Ecological Thought.* Cambridge: Harvard UP, 2010. Print.

——. *Ecology without Nature: Rethinking Environmental Aesthetics.* Cambridge: Harvard UP, 2007. Print.

Moylan, Tom. *Demand the Impossible: Science Fiction and the Utopian Imagination.* New York: Methuen, 1986. Print.

Mraović-O'Hare, Damjana. "The Beautiful, Horrifying Past: Nostalgia and Apocalypse in Don DeLillo's *Underworld*." *Criticism* 53.2 (2011): 213–39. Print.

Müller, Klaus Peter. "Re-Constructions of Reality in Margaret Atwood's Literature: A Constructionist Approach." *Margaret Atwood: Works and Impact*. Ed. Reingard M. Nischik. Rochester: Camden House, 2000. 229–58. Print.

Mumford, Lewis. *The Golden Day: A Study in American Experience and Culture*. New York: Boni and Liveright, 1926. Print.

Muntean, Nick. "Nuclear Death and Radical Hope in *Dawn of the Dead* and *On the Beach*." *Better Off Dead: The Evolution of the Zombie as Post-Human*. Ed. Deborah Christie and Sarah Juliet Lauro. New York: Fordham UP, 2011. 81–97. Print.

Murphy, Kieran M. "White Zombie." *Contemporary French and Francophone Studies* 15.1 (2011): 47–55. Print.

Murphy, Patrick D. *Ecocritical Explorations in Literary and Cultural Studies: Fences, Boundaries, and Fields*. Lanham: Lexington Books, 2010. Print.

Nadel, Alan. *Invisible Criticism: Ralph Ellison and the American Canon*. Iowa City: U of Iowa P, 1988. Print.

Nattermann, Udo. "Mundane Boundaries: Eco-Political Elements in Three Science Fiction Stories." *ISLE* 20.1 (2013): 112–24. Print.

Naydan, Liliana M. "Apocalyptic Cycles in Don DeLillo's *Underworld*." *LIT: Literature Interpretation Theory* 23.2 (2012): 179–201. Print.

Neighbors, Jim. "Plunging (outside of) History: Naming and Self-Possession in *Invisible Man*." *African American Review* 36.2 (2002): 227–42. Print.

Newbury, Michael. "Fast Zombie/Slow Zombie: Food Writing, Horror Movies, and Agribusiness Apocalypse." *American Literary History* 24.1 (2012): 87–114. Print.

Norquay, Glenda, and Gerry Smyth. *Across the Margins: Cultural Identity and Change in the Atlantic Archipelago*. Manchester: Manchester UP, 2002. Print.

Osteen, Mark. *American Magic and Dread: Don DeLillo's Dialogue with Culture*. Philadelphia: U of Pennsylvania P, 2000. Print.

Palacios, Marco. *Between Legitimacy and Violence: A History of Colombia, 1875–2002*. Durham: Duke UP, 2006. Print.

Phillips, Dana. *The Truth of Ecology: Nature, Culture, and Literature in America*. Oxford: Oxford UP, 2003. Print.

Pollard, Charles W. *New World Modernisms: T. S. Eliot, Derek Walcott, and Kamau Brathwaite*. Charlottesville: U of Virginia P, 2004. Print.

Pollock, Greg. "Undead Is the New Green: Zombies and Political Ecology." *Zombies Are Us: Essays on the Humanity of the Walking Dead*. Ed. Christopher M. Moreman and Cory Rushton. Jefferson: McFarland, 2011. 169–82. Print.

Posada-Carbó, Eduardo. "Fiction as History: The Bananeras and Gabriel García Márquez's *One Hundred Years of Solitude*." *Journal of Latin American Studies* 30.2 (1998): 395–414. Print.

Prior, Antony. "Living in Limbo." *Routes of the Roots: Geography and Literature in the English-Speaking Countries*. Ed. Isabella M. Zoppi. Rome: Bulzoni, 1998. 581–93. Print.

Pynchon, Thomas. *The Crying of Lot 49*. Philadelphia: Lippincott, 1966. Print.

——. *Gravity's Rainbow*. New York: Viking, 1973. Print.

——. "Is It O.K. to Be a Luddite?" *The New York Times on the Web*. 28 October

1984. Web. 19 November 2012. <http://www.nytimes.com/books/97/05/18/reviews/pynchon-luddite.html>.

——. *Mason & Dixon.* New York: Henry Holt, 1997. Print.

——. *V: A Novel.* Philadelphia: Lippincott, 1963. Print.

Ralph, Brian. *Daybreak.* Montreal: Drawn & Quarterly, 2011. Print.

Ramazani, Jahan. *The Hybrid Muse: Postcolonial Poetry in English.* Chicago: U of Chicago P, 2001. Print.

——. "The Wound of History: Walcott's *Omeros* and the Postcolonial Poetics of Affliction." *PMLA* 112.3 (1997): 405–17. Print.

Read, Kay A., and Jason J. González. *Mesoamerican Mythology: A Guide to the Gods, Heroes, Rituals, and Beliefs of Mexico and Central America.* Oxford: Oxford UP, 2000. Print.

Romero, George A. *Dawn of the Dead.* Troy: Anchor Bay Entertainment, 1978. Film.

——. *Night of the Living Dead.* Los Angeles: Continental Distributing, 1968. Film.

Roos, Bonnie. "Rewriting Eden in Walcott's *Omeros*: A Sea Change of Stories in Visible Silence." *Postcolonial Green: Environmental Politics and World Narratives.* Ed. Bonnie Roos and Alex Hunt. Charlottesville: UP of Virginia, 2010. 229–250. Print.

Roos, Bonnie, and Alex Hunt. *Postcolonial Green: Environmental Politics & World Narratives.* Charlottesville: UP of Virginia, 2010. Print.

Roughgarden, Joan. *Evolution's Rainbow: Diversity, Gender, and Sexuality in Nature and People.* Berkeley: U of California P, 2004. Print.

Round, Julia. "The Horror of Humanity." *The Walking Dead and Philosophy.* Ed. Wayne Yuen. Chicago: Open Court, 2012. 155–66. Print.

Rouse, David C., and Ignacio F. Bunster-Ossa. *Green Infrastructure: A Landscape Approach.* Chicago: American Planning Association, 2013. Print.

Saar, Martin, and Christian Skirke. "'The Realm of Velocity and Spleen': Reading Hybrid Life in *Mason & Dixon.*" *American Postmodernity: Essays on the Recent Fiction of Thomas Pynchon.* Ed. Ian D. Copestake. New York: Peter Lang, 2003. 129–46. Print.

"Salmon and Sterling Nuclear Test Sites." *Center for Land Use Interpretation.* 2008. Web. 10 August 2008. <http://clui.org/ludb/site/salmon-and-sterling-nuclear-test-sites>.

Saltzman, Arthur. "'Cranks of Ev'ry Radius': Romancing the Line in *Mason & Dixon.*" *Pynchon and* Mason & Dixon. Ed. Brooke Horvath and Irving Malin. Newark: U of Delaware P, 2000. 63–72. Print.

Sandilands, Catriona. "Green Things in the Garbage: Ecocritical Gleaning in Walter Benjamin's Arcades." *Ecocritical Theory: New European Approaches.* Ed. Axel Goodbody and Kate Rigby. Charlottesville: UP of Virginia, 2011. 30–42. Print.

Schaub, Thomas H. "Plot, Ideology, and Compassion in *Mason & Dixon.*" *Pynchon and* Mason & Dixon. Ed. Brooke Horvath and Irving Malin. Newark: U of Delaware P, 2000. 189–202. Print.

Seed, David. "Mapping the Course of Empire in the New World." *Pynchon and* Mason & Dixon. Ed. Brooke Horvath and Irving Malin. Newark: U of Delaware P, 2000. 84–99. Print.

Shakun, Jeremy D., Peter U. Clark, Feng He, Shaun A. Marcott, Alan C. Mix,

Zhengyu Liu, Bette Otto-Bliesner, Andreas Schmittner, and Edouard Bard. "Global Warming Preceded by Increasing Carbon Dioxide Concentrations during the Last Deglaciation." *Nature* 484 (2012): 49–54. Print.

Sharp, Patrick B. "Questing for an Indigenous Future: Leslie Marmon Silko's *Ceremony* as Indigenous Science Fiction." *Black and Brown Planets: The Politics of Race in Science Fiction.* Ed. Isiah Lavender III. Jackson: UP of Mississippi, 2014. 117–130. Print.

——. *Savage Perils: Racial Frontiers and Nuclear Apocalypse in American Culture.* Norman: U of Oklahoma P, 2007. Print.

Sheckels, Theodore F. *The Political in Margaret Atwood's Fiction: The Writing on the Wall of the Tent.* London: Ashgate, 2012. Print.

Shelley, Mary. *Frankenstein.* 1818. New York: Penguin, 1992. Print.

Shutkin, William, and Rafael Mares. "Brownfields and the Redevelopment of Communities: Linking Health, Economy, and Justice." *Reclaiming the Environmental Debate: The Politics of Health in a Toxic Culture.* Ed. Richard Hofrichter. Cambridge: MIT Press, 2000. 57–75. Print.

Singer, Marc. "'A Slightly Different Sense of Time': Palimpsestic Time in *Invisible Man.*" *Twentieth-Century Literature* 49.3 (2003): 388–419. Print.

Smith, Kimberly K. *African American Environmental Thought.* Lawrence: UP of Kansas, 2007. Print.

Song, Min Hyoung. "Becoming Planetary." *American Literary History* 23.3 (2011): 555-73. Print.

Spariosu, Mihai I. *The Wreath of Wild Olive: Play, Liminality, and the Study of Literature.* Albany: State U of New York P, 1997. Print.

Springer, Robert. *Nobody Knows Where the Blues Come From: Lyrics and History.* Jackson: UP of Mississippi, 2006. Print.

Staes, Toon. "The Enduring Stuff of Narrative: Late Capitalist Ideology and the End of History in Don DeLillo's *Underworld* and *Cosmopolis.*" *English Text Construction* 4.1 (2011): 1-17. Print.

Stein, Rachel. "Sex, Population, and Environmental Eugenics in Margaret Atwood's *Oryx and Crake* and *The Year of the Flood.*" *International Perspectives in Feminist Ecocriticism.* Ed. Greta Gaard, Simon C. Estok, and Serpil Oppermann. New York: Routledge, 2013. 184–202. Print.

Strachan, Ian G. *Paradise and Plantation: Tourism and Culture in the Anglophone Caribbean.* Charlottesville: UP of Virginia, 2002. Print.

Strandberg, Victor. "Dimming the Enlightenment: Thomas Pynchon's *Mason & Dixon.*" *Pynchon and* Mason & Dixon. Ed. Brooke Horvath and Irving Malin. Newark: U of Delaware P, 2000. 100–111. Print.

Struebig, Patricia. "Nature and Sexuality in Gabriel García Márquez's *One Hundred Years of Solitude.*" *Selecta: Journal of the Pacific Northwest Council on Foreign Languages* 15 (1984): 58–62. Print.

Tanner, Tony. "Afterthoughts on Don DeLillo's *Underworld.*" *Raritan* 17.4 (1998): 48–71. Print.

——. *The American Mystery: American Literature from Emerson to DeLillo.* Cambridge: Cambridge UP, 2000. Print.

Tekdemir, Hande. "Magical Realism in the Peripheries of the Metropolis: A Comparative Approach to *Tropic of Orange* and *Berji Kristin: Tales from the Garbage Hills.*" *Comparatist* 35.1 (2011): 40–54. Print.

Thomas, Valorie D. "'1 + 1 = 3' and Other Dilemmas: Reading Vertigo in *Invisible Man, My Life in the Bush of Ghosts,* and *Song of Solomon.*" *African American Review* 37.1 (2003): 81–94. Print.

Tittler, Jonathan. "Ecological Criticism and Spanish American Fiction: An Overview." *The Natural World in Latin American Literatures: Ecocritical Essays on Twentieth Century Writings.* Ed. Adrian T. Kane. Jefferson: McFarland, 2010. 11–36. Print.

Tsing, Anna Lowenhaupt. "Blasted Landscapes (and the Gentle Art of Mushroom Picking)." *The Multispecies Salon.* Durham: Duke UP, 2014. 87–109. Print.

Turner, Victor Witter. *Dramas, Fields, and Metaphors: Symbolic Action in Human Society.* Ithaca: Cornell UP, 1974. Print.

——. *The Forest of Symbols: Aspects of Ndembu Ritual.* Ithaca: Cornell UP, 1967. Print.

——. *From Ritual to Theatre: The Human Seriousness of Play.* New York: New York Performing Arts Journal Publications, 1982. Print.

——. *The Ritual Process: Structure and Anti-Structure.* Ithaca: Cornell UP, 1969. Print.

Twitchell, James B. *Preposterous Violence: Fables of Aggression in Modern Culture.* Oxford: Oxford UP, 1989. Print.

Vidal, Gore. *Kalki.* 1978. New York: Penguin, 1998. Print.

Viljoen, Hein, and C. N. Van der Merwe. *Beyond the Threshold: Explorations of Liminality in Literature.* New York: Peter Lang, 2007. Print.

Vint, Sherryl. *Animal Alterity: Science Fiction and the Question of the Animal.* Liverpool: Liverpool UP, 2010. Print.

——. *Bodies of Tomorrow: Technology, Subjectivity, Science Fiction.* Toronto: U of Toronto P, 2007. Print.

——. "Orange County: Global Networks in *Tropic of Orange.*" *Science Fiction Studies* 39.3 (2012): 401–14. Print.

Walcott, Derek. "The Antilles: Fragments of Epic Memory." *Nobelprize.org.* 2012. Web. 25 September 2012. <http://www.nobelprize.org/nobel_prizes/literature/laureates/1992/walcott-lecture.html>.

——. "'The Argument of the Outboard Motor': An Interview with Derek Walcott." *Caribbean Literature and the Environment: Between Nature and Culture.* Ed. Elizabeth M. DeLoughrey, Renée K. Gosson, and George B. Handley. Charlottesville: UP of Virginia, 2005. 127–39. Print.

——. *The Arkansas Testament.* New York: Farrar, Straus and Giroux, 1987. Print.

——. "Isla Incognita." *Caribbean Literature and the Environment: Between Nature and Culture.* Ed. Elizabeth M. DeLoughrey, Renée K. Gosson, and George B. Handley. Charlottesville: UP of Virginia, 2005. 51–57. Print.

——. *Omeros.* New York: Farrar, Straus and Giroux, 1990. Print.

——. "Reflections on *Omeros.*" *South Atlantic Quarterly* 96.2 (1997): 229–46. Print.

——. "What the Twilight Says: An Overture." *Dream on Monkey Mountain and Other Plays.* New York: Farrar, Straus and Giroux, 1970. 3–40. Print.

Wald, Sarah D. "'Refusing to Halt': Mobility and the Quest for Spatial Justice in Helena María Viramontes's *Their Dogs Came with Them* and Karen Tei Yamashita's *Tropic of Orange.*" *Western American Literature* 48.1–2 (2013): 70–89. Print.

Warren, Joyce W., and Margaret Dickie. *Challenging Boundaries: Gender and Periodization.* Athens: U of Georgia P, 2000. Print.

Warren, Kenneth W. *So Black and Blue: Ralph Ellison and the Occasion of Criticism.* Chicago: U of Chicago P, 2003. Print.

Washington, Booker T. *The Story of My Life and Work.* New York: Negro Universities Press, 1969. Print.

——. *Working with the Hands.* New York: Negro Universities Press, 1969. Print.

"Watts Towers Arts Center Campus." *wattstowers.org.* 2015. Web. 12 December 2015. <http://wattstowers.org>.

Weir, Lorraine. "Atwood in a Landscape." *Margaret Atwood, Language, Text, and System.* Ed. Sherrill Grace and Lorraine Weir. Vancouver: U of British Columbia P, 1983. 143–53. Print.

Weisman, Alan. *The World Without Us.* New York: Picador, 2007. Print.

West, Rinda. *Out of the Shadow: Ecopsychology, Story, and Encounters with the Land.* Charlottesville: UP of Virginia, 2007. Print.

"Whip-poor-will." *The Cornell Lab of Ornithology: All About Birds.* Cornell University. 2011. Web. 26 September 2012. <http://www.allaboutbirds.org/guide/whip-poor-will/id>.

"Wild Norway Rat Behavior." *Rat Behavior and Biology.* 2013. Web. 14 May 2013. <http://www.ratbehavior.org/WildRats.htm>.

Williams, Raymond L. "An Eco-Critical Reading of *One Hundred Years of Solitude.*" *The Cambridge Companion to Gabriel García Márquez.* Ed. Philip Swanson. Cambridge: Cambridge UP, 2010. 64–77. Print.

Williams, Tony. *The Cinema of George A. Romero: Knight of the Living Dead.* London: Wallflower, 2003. Print.

Wilson, Edward O. *Biophilia.* Cambridge: Harvard UP, 1984. Print.

——. *The Creation: An Appeal to Save Life on Earth.* New York: Norton, 2006. Print.

——. *The Future of Life.* New York: Knopf, 2002. Print.

Wisker, Gina. *Margaret Atwood: An Introduction to Critical Views of Her Fiction.* New York: Palgrave Macmillan, 2012. Print.

Wood, Wallace, Craig Yoe, Steve Banes, and Clizia Gussoni. *Zombies.* Yoe Books: IDW, 2012. Print.

Wright, John S. *Shadowing Ralph Ellison.* Jackson: UP of Mississippi, 2006. Print.

Wyke, Clement H. "The Geography of the Imagination: Spatial-Temporal Perspectives in Walcott's *Omeros.*" *Routes of the Roots: Geography and Literature in the English-Speaking Countries.* Ed. Isabella M. Zoppi. Rome: Bulzoni, 1998. 355–71. Print.

Yamashita, Karen Tei. *Tropic of Orange: A Novel.* Minneapolis: Coffee House Press, 1997. Print.

Zamora, Lois P. *Writing the Apocalypse: Historical Vision in Contemporary U.S. and Latin American Fiction.* Cambridge: Cambridge UP, 1989. Print.

Zavala, Iris M. "*One Hundred Years of Solitude* as Chronicle of the Indies." *Gabriel García Márquez's* One Hundred Years of Solitude*: A Casebook.* Ed. Gene H. Bell-Villada. Oxford: Oxford UP, 2002. 109–25. Print.

"Zombies." *The Walking Dead Wiki.* Wikia. 2013. Web. 3 April 2013. <http://walkingdead.wikia.com/wiki/Zombies>.

Zoppi, Isabella M. "*Omeros*: Derek Walcott and the Contemporary Epic Poem." *Callaloo* 22.2 (1999): 509–28. Print.

Index